Decoupled Django

Understand and Build Decoupled Django Architectures for JavaScript Front-ends

Valentino Gagliardi

Apress®

Decoupled Django: Understand and Build Decoupled Django Architectures for JavaScript Front-ends

Valentino Gagliardi
Colle di Val D'Elsa, Italy

ISBN-13 (pbk): 978-1-4842-7143-8
ISBN-13 (electronic): 978-1-4842-7144-5
https://doi.org/10.1007/978-1-4842-7144-5

Managing Director, Apress Media LLC: Welmoed Spahr
Acquisitions Editor: Celestin Suresh John
Development Editor: James Markham
Coordinating Editor: Aditee Mirashi

Cover designed by eStudioCalamar

Cover image designed by Freepik (www.freepik.com)

Distributed to the book trade worldwide by Springer Science+Business Media New York, 1 New York Plaza, Suite 4600, New York, NY 10004-1562, USA. Phone 1-800-SPRINGER, fax (201) 348-4505, e-mail orders-ny@ springer-sbm.com, or visit www.springeronline.com. Apress Media, LLC is a California LLC and the sole member (owner) is Springer Science + Business Media Finance Inc (SSBM Finance Inc). SSBM Finance Inc is a **Delaware** corporation.

For information on translations, please e-mail booktranslations@springernature.com; for reprint, paperback, or audio rights, please e-mail bookpermissions@springernature.com.

Apress titles may be purchased in bulk for academic, corporate, or promotional use. eBook versions and licenses are also available for most titles. For more information, reference our Print and eBook Bulk Sales web page at http://www.apress.com/bulk-sales.

Any source code or other supplementary material referenced by the author in this book is available to readers on GitHub via the book's product page, located at www.apress.com/978-1-4842-7143-8. For more detailed information, please visit http://www.apress.com/source-code.

Printed on acid-free paper

To my grandfather, Valentino. I will always miss you.

Table of Contents

About the Author

Valentino Gagliardi is a freelance consultant with many years of experience in the IT industry. He spent the last several years as a frontend consultant, providing advice and help, coaching, and training on JavaScript and React. He worked as an instructor for many training agencies around the country, running in-person workshops and creating learning paths for aspiring developers. Author of *The Little JavaScript Book*, he loves to share his knowledge on his blog, with his tutorials reaching over 100k monthly visits. An avid Django user, he is active in the Python community as a speaker and as a coach for Django Girls.

About the Technical Reviewer

 **Marcin Gębala** is a software engineer specializing in building web apps with Python and Django, which he has been doing professionally since 2014. He works as a staff engineer, leading the backend team, which develops the GraphQL API. He has spoken at several tech conferences, including GraphQL Summit and PyCon Korea, and his main topics of interest are open-source, Python, and GraphQL. In his free time, he is a runner, musician, and traveler. He is based in Wrocław, Poland.

Acknowledgments

This book is the product of my love for Django and its community.

I'd also like to express my gratitude to the Italian Python community in particular, one of the most welcoming out there!

Introduction

If you're reading this, I'm glad! It means you are interested in Django, one of the most powerful and flexible web frameworks out there.

When I discovered Django years ago, I realized I could make perfectly working prototypes faster than with any other web framework; prototypes that later would become robust, rock-solid web applications.

These days, with JavaScript all the rage, the temptation to jump on the JavaScript-full-stack bandwagon is strong, and sometimes this tendency makes beginners think that everything must be built with JavaScript. It shouldn't. Even if I work primarily with JavaScript, Django is still my safe harbor for building stuff quickly.

At the same time, used with cognition, modern frontend libraries like Vue.js and React pair well with Django, which can work completely decoupled from the frontend. This book is an attempt to cover a part of the vast spectrum of decoupled architectures with Django and JavaScript, with an eye on the last developments in the asynchronous Django land, and on the integration between Django and GraphQL. Here's a breakdown of what you can expect from each chapter.

- In Chapters 1, 2, and 3, we introduce the terminology, what makes a decoupled architecture, how modern JavaScript is supposed to work in Django, and how the Django REST framework can help you build REST APIs.

- In Chapter 4, we discuss the advantages and drawbacks of a decoupled architecture.

- In Chapters 5 and 6, we begin to build a Django project with the Django REST framework and Vue.js to show how Vue can work from within Django templates.

- In Chapter 7, we discuss security for REST APIs, and deployment of our Django/Vue.js project.

- In Chapter 8, we move to React and Next.js to show how such a framework can be paired with Django. We cover Next.js basics and data fetching.

- Chapter 9 covers testing, both for the REST API and for the JavaScript frontend.

- Chapter 10 covers authentication for decoupled setups and shows you how to use session-based authentication for single-page apps with the help of NGINX.

- Finally, in Chapters 11 and 12, we cover GraphQL in Django, with a look at running Django asynchronously.

All the system commands presented in this book assume that the reader is using a Linux or MacOS system. As for the prerequisites, a basic knowledge of TypeScript and modern frontend libraries is expected.

Have fun!

CHAPTER 1

Introduction to the Decoupled World

This chapter offers a brief introduction to:

- Monoliths and decoupled architectures

- REST architectures

- The GraphQL query language

In this chapter, we review traditional web applications, the classic MVC pattern based on views, models, and controllers.

We begin to outline use cases, benefits, and drawbacks of decoupled architectures. We explore the foundations of REST, look at how it compares to GraphQL, and learn that REST APIs are not only RESTful after all.

Monoliths and MVC

For at least two decades, traditional websites and applications all shared a common design based on the *Model-View-Controller* pattern, abbreviated MVC.

This pattern wasn't built in a day. In the beginning, there was an intertwined mess of business logic, HTML, and what once was a pale imitation of the JavaScript we know today. In a typical MVC arrangement, when a user requests a path to a website, the application responds with some HTML. Behind the scenes, a *controller*, usually a function or a method, takes care to return the appropriate view to the user. This happens after the controller populates the view with data coming from the database layer, most of the time, through an ORM (*object-relational mapping*). Such a system, acting as a whole to serve the user, with all its components living in a single place, is called *monolith*.

© Valentino Gagliardi 2021
V. Gagliardi, *Decoupled Django*, https://doi.org/10.1007/978-1-4842-7144-5_1

In a monolithic web application, the HTML response is generated right before returning the page to the user, a process known as traditional *server-side rendering*. Figure 1-1 shows a representation of MVC.

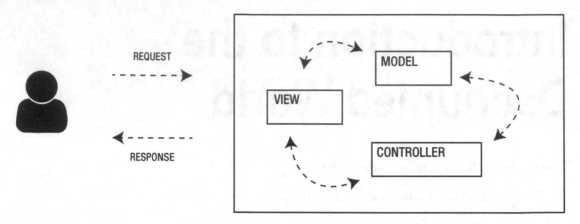

Figure 1-1. *An MVC application responds to the user with a view, generated by a controller. The model layer supplies the data from the database*

MVC has variations, like the *Model-View-Template* pattern employed by Django. In Django's MVT, the data comes still from the database, but the view acts like a controller: it gets data from the database through the ORM and injects the result in a template, which is returned to the user. MVC and its variations are well and alive: all the most popular web frameworks like .NET core, Rails, Laravel, and Django itself employ this pattern with success. However, in recent times we are seeing the spread of decoupled applications based on a *service-oriented architecture*.

In this design, a RESTful or a GraphQL API exposes data for one or more JavaScript frontends, for a mobile application, or for another machine. Service-oriented and decoupled architectures are a broader category that encompasses the galaxy of *microservices* systems. Throughout the book, we refer to decoupled architectures in the context of web applications, mainly as systems with a REST API, or GraphQL on the backend, and a separated JavaScript/HTML frontend. Before focusing on REST APIs, let's first unpack what's behind a decoupled architecture.

What Makes a Decoupled Architecture?

A *decoupled architecture* is a system that abides to one of the most important rules in software engineering: *separation of concerns*.

In a decoupled architecture, there is a clear separation between the client and the server. This is also one of the most important constraints required by REST. Figure 1-2 shows an overview of such a system, with a backend and a frontend.

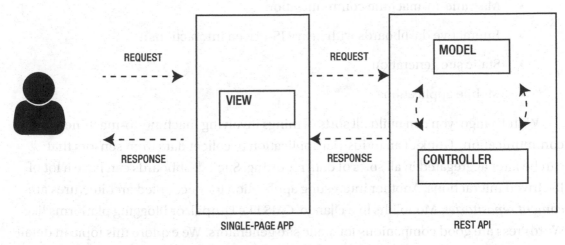

Figure 1-2. *A decoupled application with a REST API as a data source for a JavaScript/HTML frontend*

As you will see later in the book, this separation between client and server, views and controllers, is not always strict, and depending on the decoupling style, the distinction becomes blurry. For example, we can have the REST API and the frontend living in two completely different environments (separate domains or different *origins*). In this case, the division is crystal clear. In some situations, when a full JavaScript frontend would not make sense, Django can still expose a REST or GraphQL API, with JavaScript embedded in a Django template talking to the endpoints.

To muddle things further, frameworks like Angular adopt the Model-View-Controller pattern even for structuring frontend code. In a single-page application, we can find the same MVC design, which replicates the backend structure. You can already guess that one of the disadvantages of a purely decoupled architecture is, to some extent, code duplication. Having defined what is a decoupled architecture, let's now talk about its use cases.

Why and When to Decouple?

This isn't a book about the JavaScript gold rush. In fact, you should weigh your options long before thinking about a full rewrite of your beloved Django monolith.

Not every project needs a single-page application. If instead your application falls under one of the following categories, you can start evaluating the advantages of a decoupled architecture. Here's a list of the most common use cases:

- Machine-to-machine communication

- Interactive dashboards with heavy JS-driven interactions

- Static site generation

- Mobile applications

With Django, you can build all sorts of things involving machine-to-machine communication. Think of an industrial application to collect data from sensors that can be later aggregated in all sorts of data reporting. Such dashboards can have a lot of JS-driven interactions. Another interesting application for decoupled architectures are *content repositories*. Monoliths like Django, CMS like Drupal, or blogging platforms like WordPress are good companions for static site generators. We explore this topic in detail later.

Another benefit of a decoupled architecture is the ability to serve different types of clients: mobile applications are one of the most compelling use cases. Now, if decoupled architectures sound too appealing, I advise you to consider their drawbacks. Decoupled architectures based exclusively on single-page applications are not always a valid choice for:

- Constrained teams

- Websites with little or no JS-driven interactions

- Constrained devices

- Content-heavy websites with search engine optimization in mind

---

Note   As you will see in Chapter 7, frameworks like Next.js can help with search engine optimization for single-page apps by producing static HTML. Other examples of frameworks employing this technique are Gatsby and Prerenderer.

It's easy to get overwhelmed by modern frontend development, especially if the team is small. One of the most serious hindrances when designing or building a decoupled architecture from scratch is the sheer amount of complexity lurking behind the surface of JavaScript tooling. In the next sections, we focus on REST and GraphQL, the two pillars of a decoupled architecture.

Hypermedia All the Things

The foundation for almost any decoupled frontend architecture is the *REST architectural style*.

REST is hardly a novel concept these days. The theory is that through *verbs* or commands, we create, retrieve, or modify *resources* on a system. For example, given a User model on the backend, exposed by a REST API as a resource, we can get a collection of all the instances present in the database with a GET HTTP request. The following shows a typical GET request to retrieve a list of entities:

```
GET https://api.example/api/users/
```

As you can see, we say users, not user, when retrieving the resource. As a convention, resources should always be plural. To retrieve a single resource from the API, we pass instead the ID in the path, as a *path parameter*. The following shows a GET request to a single resource:

```
GET https://api.example/api/users/1
```

Table 1-1 shows a breakdown of all the verbs (HTTP methods) and their effect on the resources.

Table 1-1. *HTTP Methods with the Corresponding Effect on a Given Resource Present on the Backend*

Method	Effect	Idempotent
POST	Create resource	No
GET	Retrieve resource(s)	Yes
PUT	Update resource	Yes
DELETE	Delete resource	Yes
PATCH	Partial update resource	No

To refer to this set of HTTP methods we also use the term *CRUD*, which stands for Create, Read, Update, and Delete. As you can see from the table, some HTTP verbs are *idempotent*, meaning that the result of the operation is always stable. A GET request for example always returns the same data, no matter how many times we issue the command after the first request. A POST request instead will always induce a side effect, that is, create a new resource on the backend with different values for each call. When retrieving a resource with GET, we can use *search parameters* in a query string to specify search constraints, sorting, or to limit the number of results. The following shows a request for a limited set of users:

```
GET https://api.example/api/users?limit=20
```

When creating a new resource with POST instead, we can send a *request body* alongside the request. Depending on the operation type, the API can respond with an HTTP status code, and with the newly created object. Common examples of HTTP response code are 200 OK and 201 Created, 202 Accepted. When things don't go well, the API might respond with an error code. Common examples of HTTP error codes are 500 Internal Server Error, 403 Forbidden, and 401 Unauthorized.

This back and forth communication between the client and the server carries JSON objects over the HTTP protocol. Nowadays, JSON is the preferred format for exchanging data, whereas in the past you could have seen XML over HTTP (SOAP architectures are still alive these days). Why does REST follow these conventions, and why does it use HTTP? When Roy Fielding wrote his dissertation entitled, "Architectural Styles and the Design of Network-based Software Architectures" in 2000, he defined the following rules:

- *Hypermedia as the engine*: When requesting a resource, the response from the APIs must also include hyperlinks to related entities or to other actions.

- *Client-server separation*: The consumer (JavaScript, a machine, or a generic client) and the Web API must be two separate entities.

- *Stateless*: The communication between client and server should not use any data stored on the server.

- *Cacheable*: The API should leverage HTTP caching as much as possible.

- *Uniform interface*: The communication between client and server should use a representation of the resources involved, and a standard language for the communication.

It's worth taking a quick detour to dive deeper into each of these rules.

Hypermedia as the Engine

In the original dissertation, this constraint is buried under the *Uniform Interface* section, but it's crucial for understanding the real nature of REST APIs.

What hypermedia as the engine means in practice is that when communicating with an API, we should be able to see what's next by examining any link in the response. Django REST framework, the most popular framework for building REST APIs in Django, makes it easy to build *Hypermedia APIs*. In fact, Django REST framework serializers have the ability to return *hyperlinked resources*. For example, a query for a List model can return the *many* side of a *one-to-many* relationship. Listing 1-1 illustrates a JSON response from an API where the Card model is connected with a foreign key to List.

Listing 1-1. A JSON Response with Hyperlinked Relationships

```
{
  "id": 8,
  "title": "Doing",
  "cards": [
      "https://api.example/api/cards/1",
      "https://api.example/api/cards/2",
      "https://api.example/api/cards/3",
      "https://api.example/api/cards/4"
  ]
}
```

Other examples of hyperlinked resources are pagination links. Listing 1-2 is a JSON response for a boards resource (Board model) with hyperlinks for navigating between results.

Listing 1-2. A JSON Response with Pagination Links

```
{
  "id": 4,
  "title": "Doing",
  "next": "https://api.example/api/boards/?page=5",
  "previous": "https://api.example/api/boards/?page=3"
}
```

Another interesting feature of the Django REST framework is the browsable API, a web interface for interacting with the REST API. All these features make Django REST framework Hypermedia APIs ready, which is the correct definition for these systems.

Client-Server Separation

The second constraint, client-server separation, is easily achievable.

A REST API can expose endpoints to which consumers can connect to retrieve, update, or delete data. In our case, consumers will be JavaScript frontends.

Stateless

A compliant REST API should be *stateless*.

Stateless means that during the communication between client and server, the request should not use any context data stored on the server. This doesn't mean that we can't interact with the resources exposed by the REST APIs. The constraint applies to session data, like session cookies or other means of identification stored on the server. This strict prescription urged engineers to find new solutions for API authentication. JSON Web Token, referred to as JWT later in the book, is a product of such research, which is not necessarily more secure than other methods, as you will see later.

Cacheable

A compliant REST API should take advantage of HTTP caching as much as possible.

HTTP caching operates through HTTP headers. A well-designed REST API should always give the client hints about the lifetime of a GET response. To do so, the backend sets a Cache-Control header on the response with a max-age directive, which drives the lifespan of the response. For example, to cache a response for one hour, the server can set the following header:

```
Cache-Control: max-age=3600
```

Most of the time, there is also an `ETag` header in the response, which indicates the resource version. Listing 1-3 shows a typical HTTP response with cache headers.

Listing 1-3. An HTTP Response with Cache Headers

```
200 OK
Cache-Control: max-age=3600
ETag: "x6ty2xv"
```

Note   Another method for enabling HTTP caching involves the `Last-Modified` header. If the server sets this header, the client can in turn use `If-Modified-Since` or `If-Unmodified-Since` to check the resource's freshness.

When the client requests the same resource and `max-age` is not yet expired, the response is fetched from the browser's cache, not from the server. If `max-age` has expired, the client issues a request to the server by attaching the `If-None-Match` header, alongside with the value from the `ETag`. This mechanism is known as a *conditional request*. If the resource is still fresh, the server responds with `304 Not Modified`, hence avoiding unnecessary exchange of data. If the resource instead is stale, that is, it's expired, the server responds with a fresh response. It's important to remember that browsers cache only the following response codes:

- `200 OK`
- `301 Moved Permanently`
- `404 Not Found`
- `206 Partial Content`

Moreover, responses with the `Authorization` header set aren't cached by default, unless the `Cache-Control` header includes the `public` directive. Also, as you will see later, GraphQL operates mainly with `POST` requests, which aren't cached by default.

Uniform Interface

Uniform interface is one of the most important rules of REST.

One of its tenets, *representations,* prescribes that the communication between client and server, for example to create a new resource on the backend, should carry the representation of the resource itself. What this means is that if I want to create a new resource on the backend, and I issue a POST request, I should provide a payload with the resource.

Let's say I have an API that accepts a command on an endpoint, but without a *request body*. A REST API that creates a new resource based only on a command issued against an endpoint is not RESTful. If we talk in terms of uniform interface and representations instead, when we want to create a new resource on the server, we send the resource itself in the request body. Listing 1-4 illustrates a complaint request, with a request body for creating a new user.

Listing 1-4. A POST Request

```
POST https://api.example/api/users/

{
  "name": "Juliana",
  "surname": "Crain",
  "age": 44
}
```

Here we use JSON as the media type, and a representation of the resource as the request body. Uniform interface refers also to the HTTP verbs used to drive the communication from the client to the server. When we talk to a REST API, we mainly use five methods: GET, POST, PUT, DELETE, and PATCH. These methods are also the uniform interface, that is, the common language we use for client-server communication. After reviewing REST principles, let's now turn our attention to its alleged contender, GraphQL.

An Introduction to GraphQL

GraphQL appeared in 2015, proposed by Facebook, and marketed as a replacement for REST.

GraphQL is a data query language that allows the client to precisely define what data to fetch from the server and combine data from multiple resources in one request. In a sense, this is what we always did with REST APIs, but GraphQL takes this a step further, pushing more control to the client. We saw how to request data from a REST API. To get a single user, for example, we can visit the following URL of a fictional REST API:

```
https://api.example/api/users/4
```

In response, the API returns all the fields for the given user. Listing 1-5 shows a JSON response for a single user, which also happens to have a one-to-many relationship with a Friend model.

Listing 1-5. A JSON Response from a REST API

```
{
  "id": 4,
  "name": "Juliana",
  "surname": "Crain",
  "age": 44,
  "city": "London",
  "occupation": "Software developer",
  "friends": [
      "https://api.example/api/friend/1",
      "https://api.example/api/friend/2",
      "https://api.example/api/friend/3",
      "https://api.example/api/friend/4"
  ]
}
```

This is a contrived example, but if you imagine an even larger set of fields in the response, it becomes clear that we are *over-fetching*, that is, we are requesting more data than we need. If we think for a moment of the same API, this time implemented with GraphQL, we can request a smaller subset of fields. To request data from a GraphQL API,

11

we can make a *query*. Listing 1-6 shows a typical GraphQL query to request a single user, by ID, with only a subset of fields.

Listing 1-6. A GraphQL Query

```
query {
    getUser(userID: 4) {
        surname,
        age
    }
}
```

As you can see, the client controls what fields it can request. Here, for example, we skipped all fields except surname and age. This query has also an *argument* identified by userID, which acts as a first filter for the query. In response to this query, the GraphQL API returns the requested fields. Listing 1-7 shows the JSON response for our query.

Listing 1-7. A JSON Response from the Previous Query

```
{
  "surname": "Crain",
  "age": 44
}
```

"No more over-fetching" is one of the main selling points for GraphQL over REST. In reality, this filtering capability based on fields is not an exclusive of GraphQL APIs. For example, REST APIs that follow the JSON API specification can use *sparse fieldsets* to request only a subset of data. Once we issue a query against a GraphQL endpoint, this query travels over a POST request as a request body. Listing 1-8 shows a request to a GraphQL API.

Listing 1-8. A GraphQL Query over a POST Request

```
POST https://api.example/graphql

{
"query" : "query { getUser(userID: 4) { surname, age } }",
"variables": null
}
```

You can already notice in this request that we call the `/graphql` endpoint instead of `/api/users/4`. Also, we use `POST` instead of `GET` to retrieve the resource. This is a large departure from the REST architectural style. Query requests in GraphQL are only half of the story. Whereas REST uses `POST`, `PUT`, and `DELETE` to create, update, or remove a resource, respectively, GraphQL has the concept of *mutations* as a means of altering the data. Listing 1-9 shows a mutation for creating a new a user.

Listing 1-9. A GraphQL Mutation

```
mutation {
    createUser(name: "Caty", surname: "Jonson") {
        name,
        surname
    }
}
```

Subscriptions are another interesting feature of GraphQL services. Clients can subscribe to events. For example, we may want to receive a notification from the server any time a new user registers to our service. In GraphQL, we register a subscription for this. Listing 1-10 illustrates a subscription.

Listing 1-10. A GraphQL Subscription

```
subscription {
    userRegistered {
        name,
        email
    }
}
```

What happens when a GraphQL query reaches the backend? How does the flow compare to a REST API? Once the query lands on the backend, it is validated against a *schema*, which contains *type definitions*. Then one or more *resolvers*, dedicated functions connected to each field in the schema, assemble and return the appropriate data for the user. Speaking of type definitions, everything is a type in GraphQL: queries, mutations, subscriptions, and the domain entities. Each query, mutation, and entity has to be defined in a schema before it can be used, written in a *Schema Definition Language*. Listing 1-11 shows a simple schema for the queries we have seen so far.

Listing 1-11. A Simple GraphQL Schema

```
type User {
    name: String,
    surname: String,
    age: Int,
    email: String
}

type Query {
    getUser(userID: ID): User!
}

type Mutation {
    createUser(name: String, surname: String): User
}

type Subscription {
    userRegistered: User
}
```

By looking at this schema, you can immediately notice how GraphQL enforces strong types, much like a typed language like TypeScript or C#. Here, String, Int, and ID are *scalar types*, while User is our custom type. These custom types go under the definition of *object types* in GraphQL parlance. How does GraphQL fit in the Python ecosystem? Nowadays, there are a number of libraries for building Pythonesque GraphQL APIs. The most popular are as follows:

- Graphene, with its *code-first* approach to building GraphQL services

- Ariadne, a *schema-first* GraphQL library

- Strawberry, built on top of data classes, code-first, and with type hints

All these libraries have integrations with Django. The difference between a code-first approach and a schema-first approach to GraphQL is that the former promotes Python syntax as a first-class citizen for writing the schema. The latter instead uses a multi-line Python string to represent it. In Chapters 10 and 11, we work extensively with GraphQL in Django with Ariadne and Strawberry.

Summary

This chapter reviewed the fundamentals for both traditional and decoupled architectures. You learned that:

- Monoliths are systems acting as a whole unit to serve HTML and data to the users

- REST APIs are in reality Hypermedia APIs because they use HTTP as the communication medium, and hyperlinks for providing paths to related resources

- JavaScript-first and single-page apps are not the perfect solution to every use case

- GraphQL is a strong contender for REST

In the next chapter, we dive deep into the JavaScript ecosystem to see how it fits within Django.

Additional Resources

- REST, Hypermedia & HATEOAS
- HTTP Caching tutorial

CHAPTER 2

JavaScript Meets Django

This chapter covers:

- How JavaScript fits into Django

- JavaScript ecosystem and tooling

- JavaScript frontend libraries and frameworks

Despite its reputation of being a toy language, JavaScript has become a mature tool in recent years.

For bad or good, JavaScript is everywhere these days. JavaScript tooling has grown exponentially as well, with new libraries and techniques pouring fast in the ecosystem. In this chapter, we introduce the modern JavaScript scene. You will understand what JavaScript tools do, and how they fit within Django. We also take a look at the most popular frontend libraries and frameworks.

JavaScript and Django in Production

To better understand how modern JavaScript fits into Django, we should think not only of a local development environment, but first and foremost of the typical production context.

Django in production is a different beast from its development counterpart. First, Django in development has a local server that can serve static files, that is, JavaScript, images, and CSS. However, the same development server can't handle production loads, let alone the security around a production setup. For this reason, in a production environment, we usually employ the following components:

- The Django project itself

- A *reverse proxy*, such as NGINX, to serve static files, which also acts as an SSL termination

- A *WSGI* or *ASGI* server, such as Gunicorn, Uvicorn, or Hypercorn (more on ASGI in the next chapter)

17

© Valentino Gagliardi 2021
V. Gagliardi, *Decoupled Django*, https://doi.org/10.1007/978-1-4842-7144-5_2

How does JavaScript fit into this? When we deploy Django on a production server, we run `python manage.py collectstatic` to group static files for all the Django apps in a single place, identified by the `STATIC_ROOT` configuration variable. To put things in context, suppose we have a Django project with an app named quote and a JavaScript file in `~/repo-root/quote/static/quote/js/index.js`. Assuming we configured `STATIC_ROOT` as follows, where `/home/user/static/` is an existing folder on the production server:

```
STATIC_ROOT = "/home/user/static/"
```

When we run `python manage.py collectstatic`, static files land in `/home/user/static/`, ready to get picked up by any Django template that references the `static` template tag. For this to work, the `STATIC_URL` configuration must point to the URL used for serving static files. In our example, we imagine a subdomain named `static.decoupled-django.com`:

```
STATIC_URL = "https://static.decoupled-django.com/"
```

This URL is usually served by an NGINX virtual host, with a `location` block pointing at the value configured in Django's `STATIC_ROOT`. Listing 2-1 illustrates how you would call a static file (JavaScript in this case) from a Django template.

Listing 2-1. A Django Template Referencing a Static File

```
{% load static %}
<!DOCTYPE html>
<html lang="en">
<body>
<h1>Hello Django!</h1>
<div id="root"></div>
</body>
<script src="{% static "quote/js/index.js" %}"></script>
</html>
```

In the actual HTML, the URL becomes:

```
<script src="https://static.decoupled-django.com/quote/js/index.js"></script>
```

This is the most simple situation, where we have one or more Django apps, each with its own JavaScript files. This approach works well for tiny apps, where the JavaScript code for the *entry point* of the application fits within the 200KB limit. By entry point in this context, we mean the first JavaScript file that the browser has to download to kickstart the whole application. Since this book is about "decoupled Django" we need to think about more complex setups where the JavaScript payload served to the user could go well over 200KB. Also, the bigger a JavaScript application grows, the more we need to structure our code in a modular fashion, which leads us to talk about JavaScript ES modules and *module bundlers*.

The Need for Module Bundlers

Up until 2015, JavaScript didn't have a standard module system on the frontend. Whereas Node.js always had `require()` from the beginning, the situation was really scattered on the frontend with different and competing approaches like AMD modules, UMD, and CommonJS.

Finally, in 2015, *ES modules* landed in ECMAScript. ES modules offer a standard approach to code reuse in JavaScript, while also enabling powerful patterns like *dynamic import* for improving performances in bigger applications. Now, the problem for a typical frontend project is that ES modules are not the only asset available to the developer. There are images, style files such as CSS or SASS, and different types of JavaScript modules to include. Let's also not forget that ES modules are a rather new artifact, and traditional module formats are still out there. A JavaScript project might use new libraries based on ES modules, but need as well to include code distributed as CommonJS. Moreover, ES modules are not supported by older browsers.

Another challenge for modern frontend developers lies in the size of a typical JavaScript application, especially when the project requires a lot of dependencies. To overcome these issues, specialized tools known as *module bundlers* saw the light. The goals of a module bundler are manifold. This tool can:

- Assemble different types of JavaScript modules into the same application

- Include different types of files and assets in a JavaScript project

- Improve the performance of the application with a technique known as *code splitting*

In brief, module bundlers offer a unified interface for collecting all the dependencies of a frontend project, assembling them, and producing one or more JavaScript files called *bundles*, in addition to any other asset (CSS and images) for the final application. One of the most popular module bundlers these days is *webpack*, which is also used in the most important CLI tools for project scaffolding in the JavaScript land (create-react-app, Vue CLI). In the next section, we explore why webpack is important for the Django developer who needs to deal with a lot of JavaScript.

Webpack Fights Django (the Need for Code Splitting)

Code splitting in JavaScript refers to the ability to serve the minimum amount possible of JavaScript to the client, while loading all the rest on-demand.

An understanding of code splitting is not strictly necessary for the average Django developer, but Python teams approaching medium to bigger Django projects that require a lot of interactivity in the frontend must know about this concept. In the previous sections, I mentioned a theoretical limit of 200KB for the entry point of a JavaScript application. Near to this number, we risk offering a terrible navigation experience. JavaScript has a cost for any device, but the performance degradation becomes even more dramatic on low-end devices and slow networks (I suggest always keeping an eye on "The Cost of JavaScript" by Addy Osmani, link in the resources). For this reason, it's of utmost importance to apply a series of techniques to the final artifact. One such technique is *code minification,* where the final JavaScript code is stripped out of comments, whitespace, and `while` functions, and variable names are mangled. This is a well-known optimization that almost any tool can accomplish. But a more powerful technique, exclusive of modern module bundlers, called *code splitting*, can shrink down the resulting JavaScript files even more. Code splitting in a JavaScript application applies at various levels:

- At the route level

- At the component level

- On user interactions (dynamic import)

To some extent, CLI tools like Vue CLI and create-react-app already offer sane defaults out of the box when it comes to code splitting. In these tools, webpack is already configured to produce efficient output, thanks to a basic form of code splitting known as *vendor splitting*. The effect of code splitting on a JavaScript application is visible in the following example. This is the result of running `npm run build` on a minimal project configured as a single-page application:

```
js/chunk-vendors.468a5298.js
js/app.24e08b96.js
```

Subsequent slices of the application, called *chunks*, land in different files than the main entry point, and can be loaded in parallel. You can see here that we have two files, `app.24e08b96.js` and `chunk-vendors.468a5298`. The `js`. `app.24e08b96.js` file is the entry point of the application. When the application loads, the entry point requires the second chunk, named `chunk-vendors.468a5298.js`. When you see *vendors* in a chunk name, it's a sign that webpack is doing the most basic form of code splitting: vendor splitting. Vendor dependencies are libraries like lodash and React, which are potentially included in multiple places across a project. To prevent dependency duplication, webpack can be instructed to recognize what is in common between the consumers of a dependency, and splits the common dependencies into single chunks. Another thing you can notice from these file names is the hash. In `app.24e08b96.js`, for example, the hash is `24e08b96`, which is calculated from the file content by the module bundler. When the content of the file changes, the hash changes as well. The important thing to keep in mind is that the order in which the entry point and the chunks appear in the script tag is paramount for the app to work. Listing 2-2 shows how our files should appear in the HTML markup.

Listing 2-2. Two Chunks As They Appear in the HTML

```
<-- rest of the document -->
<script src=/js/chunk-vendors.468a5298.js></script>
<script src=/js/app.24e08b96.js></script>
<-- rest of the document -->
```

Here, `chunk-vendors.468a5298.js` must come before `app.24e08b96.js`, because `chunk-vendors.468a5298.js` contains one or more dependencies for the entry point. Keeping our focus on Django, you can imagine that to inject these chunks in the same exact order, we need some system for pairing the appearance order of each file with the `static` tag in our templates. A Django library called `django-webpack-loader` was meant to ease the usage of webpack within Django projects, but when webpack 4 came out with a new configuration for code splitting, `splitChunks`, `django-webpack-loader` stopped working.

The takeaway here is that JavaScript tooling moves faster than anything else, and it's not easy for package maintainers to keep up with the latest changes. Also, messing up with the webpack configuration is a luxury not everybody can afford, not counting the risk of configuration drift and breaking changes. When in doubt, before fighting webpack or touching its configuration, use this mini-heuristic to decide what to do: if the JavaScript section of an app is over 200KB, use the appropriate CLI tooling and serve the application as a single-page app within a Django template, or as a decoupled SPA. We will explore the first approach in Chapter 5. If the JavaScript code fits within the 200KB limit instead, and the amount of interactive interactions are low, use a simple `<script>` tag to load what you need, or if you want to use modern JavaScript, configure a simple webpack pipeline with vendor splitting at least. Having outlined the foundations of module bundlers, let's now continue our tour of the modern JavaScript tooling.

Note   JavaScript tooling, and webpack in particular, are too much of a moving target to cover in a book without the risk of providing outdated instructions. For this reason, I don't cover the setup of a webpack project here. You can find a link to an example of such a setup in the resources.

Modern JavaScript, Babel, and Webpack

As developers we are quite fortunate, because most of the time we have access to fast Internet connections, powerful machines with many cores, plenty of RAM, and modern browsers.

If this shiny new snippet of JavaScript works on my machine, then it should work virtually everywhere, right? It's easy to understand the appeal of writing modern JavaScript. Consider the following example, based on ECMAScript 5:

```
var arr = ["a", "b"];
function includes(arr, element) {
  return arr.indexOf(element) !== -1;
}
```

This function checks if a given element is present in an array. It is based on `Array.prototype.indexOf()`, a built-in function for arrays, which returns `-1` if the given element is not found in the target list. Now consider instead the following snippet, based on ECMAScript 2016:

```
const arr = ["a", "b"];
const result = arr.includes("c");
```

The second example is clearly more concise, understandable, and palatable for developers. The drawback is that older browsers don't understand `Array.prototype.includes()` or `const`. We can't ship this code as it is.

Tip   Both `caniuse.com` and the compatibility tables at `developer.mozilla.org` are invaluable resources for understanding if a given target browser supports modern syntax.

Luckily, fewer and fewer developers need to worry about the dreaded Internet Explorer 11, but there are still a lot of edge cases to take into account. As of today, the most compatible JavaScript version is ECMAScript 2009 (ES5), which is a safe target. To keep both JavaScript developers and users happy, the community came up with a category of tools called *transpilers*, of which Babel is the most popular incarnation. With such a tool at our disposal, we can write modern JavaScript code, pass it into a transpilation/compilation pipeline, and have compatible JavaScript code as the final product. In a typical setup, we configure a build pipeline where:

1. Webpack ingests ES modules written in modern JavaScript.

2. A webpack loader passes the code through Babel.

3. Babel transpiles the code.

The webpack/Babel duo is ubiquitous these days, used by create-react-app, Vue CLI, and more.

A Word on TypeScript

TypeScript is the elephant in the room for most developers.

As a statically typed declination of JavaScript, TypeScript is more similar to languages like C# or Java. It is widespread in the Angular world, and it is conquering more and more JavaScript libraries, which now ship with type definitions by default. Whether you like TypeScript or not, it is a tool to keep in consideration. In Chapters 8, 11, and 12, we work with TypeScript in React.

JavaScript Frontend Libraries and Frameworks

The JavaScript landscape has changed dramatically over the years. jQuery still owns a large market share.

But when it comes to client-side applications, these are being written or rewritten with modern frontend libraries like React and Vue.js, or full-fledged frameworks like Angular. Django is mostly powered by HTML templates, but when the time comes it can be paired with virtually any JavaScript library. These days the scene is dominated by three competitors:

- React, the UI library from Facebook, which popularized (but not pioneered) a component-based approach to writing interfaces

- Vue.js, the progressive UI library from Evan You, former Angular developer, which shines for its progressiveness

- Angular, the battery-included framework, based on TypeScript

Of this trio, Vue.js is the most progressive. Angular has more batteries included (just like Django), but has a steep learning curve. React instead is the most liberal because it does not impose any constraint on the developer. You pick whatever library you need. Whether this is an advantage or not, I leave the opinion for you. What is important to keep in mind is that the core UI library is just the starting point for a number of dependencies to solve another set of problems that arise when writing medium to bigger client-side applications. In particular, you will sooner or later need:

- A state management library

- A routing library

- A schema validation library

- A form validation library

Each UI library has its own orbit of satellite sub-libraries to handle the aforementioned concerns. React leans on Redux or Mobx (and more recently also on Recoil.js) for state management, and on React Router for routing. Vue.js uses Vuex for state management, and Vue Router for routing. Angular has a bunch of different approaches to state management, but NgRx is the most widespread. Ultimately, all these libraries and frameworks can work well as external clients for Django, paired either as:

- Client-side applications fetching data from a Django REST/GraphQL API

- Server-side rendered or static site generators with Django as a content source

We explore both topics in more detail later in the book. In the next section, we take a quick look at some alternatives to the traditional single-page approach.

Lightweight JavaScript UI Libraries

Other than Angular, Vue, React, and Svelte, there is a growing number of lightweight JavaScript mini-frameworks, born to ease the most mundane tasks on the frontend and to provide just enough JavaScript to get going.

In this category we can mention the following tools:

- AlpineJS

- Hotwire

- Htmx

Hotwire is a set of tooling and techniques popularized by Ruby on Rails and its creator, David Heinemeier Hansson. At the time of this writing, there is experimental work called *turbo-django* aiming at porting these techniques into Django. Along the same lines there is also a new Django framework called *django-unicorn*. All these tools offer a less JavaScript-heavy approach to building interactive interfaces. They will be worth a look once they start to gain traction in the wild.

Universal JavaScript Applications

Node.js is an environment for running JavaScript code outside of browsers. This means servers and CLI tools.

The majority of the tools we mentioned in this chapter are JavaScript-based, and since they run on the command line, they need a JavaScript environment, which Node.js provides. Now, if you pair this with frontend libraries that are capable of running on any JavaScript environment, not only browsers (like React and Vue.js), you obtain a particular breed of JavaScript tooling that is taking the scene by storm with a JavaScript-centric approach to server-side rendering.

We already mentioned server-side rendering in Chapter 1, when talking about MVC web frameworks. In contrast to traditional server-side rendering, where the HTML and the data is generated by a server-side language like Ruby, Python, or Java, in the JavaScript-centric approach to server-side rendering, everything is generated by JavaScript on Node.js. What does this mean for the end user and for the developer? The main difference between a client-side application based on JavaScript and a server-side rendered app is that the latter generates the HTML before sending it to the user, or to the search engine crawler. This approach has a number of advantages over pure client-side applications:

- It improves SEO for content-heavy websites

- It improves performances, since the main rendering effort is pushed to the server

For the developer instead, universal JavaScript applications are the holy grail of code reuse since everything can be written in a single language, JavaScript. The reasoning behind these tools and the motivations for using them are roughly the following:

- We already have a big client-side app and we want to improve its performances, both for the end user and for crawlers

- We have a lot of common code between the frontend and the Node.js backend, and we want to reuse it

However, as with any technology, universal JavaScript applications have their own drawbacks. For a Django shop focused on Python and maybe a sprinkle of JavaScript with React or Vue.js, maintaining a parallel architecture based on Node.js can be taxing. These setups need a Node.js server in order to run, with all the maintenance burden and complexity it entails. Platforms like Vercel and Netlifly ease the deployments of these architectures, but there are still things to keep in mind. The most popular tools available today for creating universal JavaScript applications are:

- Next.js for React

- Nuxt.js for Vue.js

- Angular Universal for Angular

There are probably a million more tools out there. In Chapter 7, we focus on Next.js.

Static Site Generators

While the approach to server-side rendering offered by tools like Next.js and Nuxt.js is indeed interesting, static site generation should be the first choice in all those cases where search engine optimization is paramount and there is little to no JavaScript-driven interaction on certain pages (think of a blog, for example).

The current scenario for static site generation with JavaScript includes:

- Gatsby

- Next.js for React

- Nuxt.js for Vue.js

- Scully for Angular

Next.js and Nuxt.js can work in two modes: *server-side rendering* and *static site generation*. To source data from the backend, these tools offer interfaces for making plain HTTP requests to a REST API, or alternatively GraphQL. Gatsby instead makes exclusive use of GraphQL, and might not be the right tool for every team.

Testing Tooling

The whole Chapter 8 is devoted to testing Django and JavaScript applications. In this section, we briefly introduce the most popular testing tools for JavaScript. They fall into the conventional categorizations of testing.

Unit testing:

- Jest

End-to-end testing:

- Cypress

- Puppeteer by Google

- Playwright by Microsoft

For unit testing and integration testing between multiple units, Jest is the most popular tool to this date. It can test pure JavaScript code and React/Vue.js components as well. For end-to-end testing and functional testing, Cypress is the most feature-complete test runner, and plays well with Django too, with Puppeteer and Playwright gaining traction. Truth be told, Jest and Cypress can be thought more as wrappers around existing testing libraries: Jest builds on top of Jasmine, while Cypress builds on top of Mocha, as they borrow a high number of methods from these libraries. However, their popularity is sparked by the fluent testing API they provide, in contrast to more traditional tools.

Other Ancillary JavaScript Tools

I would be remiss not to mention ancillary JavaScript tools, so important for the modern JavaScript developer.

In both the Python and JavaScript land, there are code linters. For JavaScript, ESLint is the most widespread. Then we have code formatters like Prettier. At the intersection between pure JavaScript code and design systems we find Storybook, a powerful tool for building design systems. Storybook is used widely in the React and React Native community, but compatible with the most popular frontend libraries like Vue and Svelte. Together with testing tools, linters, formatters, and UI tools make a powerful arsenal for every JavaScript and Django developer.

Summary

This chapter explored the boundaries of Django and client-side applications. You learned about:

- JavaScript and Django in production

- Module bundlers and code splitting

- How webpack integrates into Django

- JavaScript tooling as a whole

- Universal JavaScript applications

In the next chapter, we introduce the asynchronous Django landscape.

Additional Resources

- The cost of JavaScript

- Setting up React and webpack within a Django project

CHAPTER 3

Modern Django and the Django REST Framework

This chapter covers:

- The Django REST framework and Django side by side
- Asynchronous Django

I guess all Django developers share a common story. They built a lot of stuff and tried the mini-framework approach à la Flask, but in the end, they always returned to Django simply because it is opinionated, and it offers all the tools for building full-stack web applications with Python. The Django REST Framework is a Django package that follows the same pragmatic approach. In this chapter, we compare the Django REST Framework to Django, and we explore the asynchronous Django landscape.

What Is the Django REST Framework?

The Django REST Framework (DRF for short) is a Django package for building Web APIs.

Despite the rapid spread of GraphQL and the emergence of asynchronous micro-frameworks like Starlette and FastAPI, the DRF still powers thousands of web services. The DRF integrates seamlessly with Django to complement its features for building REST APIs. In particular it offers an array of ready-made components:

- Class-based REST views
- Viewsets
- Serializers

© Valentino Gagliardi 2021
V. Gagliardi, *Decoupled Django*, https://doi.org/10.1007/978-1-4842-7144-5_3

This chapter isn't intended as a guide to the DRF for beginners, but it is worth spending some words to go over the main building blocks of this package. In the next sections, we explore these components, since they will be the Lego blocks for the first part of our decoupled Django project.

Class-Based Views in Django and the DRF

When building web applications, some common patterns for handling data insertion and data listing repeat over and over.

Consider an HTML form for example. There are three distinct phases to take account of:

- Displaying the form, either empty or with initial data

- Validating the user input and showing eventual errors

- Saving the data to the database

It would be foolish to copy-paste the same code again and again in our projects. For this reason, Django offers a convenient abstraction around common patterns in web development. These classes go under the name of *class-based view*, or *CBV* for short. Some examples of CBV in Django are `CreateView`, `ListView`, `DeleteView`, `UpdateView`, and `DetailView`. As you might have noticed, the naming of these classes goes hand in hand with the CRUD pattern, so common in REST APIs and in traditional web applications. In particular:

- `CreateView` and `UpdateView` for POST requests

- `ListView` and `DetailView` for GET requests

- `DeleteView` for DELETE requests

The Django REST Framework follows the same convention and offers a wide toolbox of class-based views for REST API development:

- `CreateAPIView` for POST requests

- `ListAPIView` and `RetrieveAPIView` for GET requests

- `DestroyAPIView` for DELETE requests

- `UpdateAPIView` for PUT and PATCH requests

In addition, you can peruse a combination of CBVs for retrieve/delete operations like `RetrieveDestroyAPIView`, or for retrieve/update/destroy like `RetrieveUpdateDestroyAPIView`. You will use a lot of these CBVs in your decoupled Django projects to speed up development of the most common tasks, although the DRF offers a more powerful layer on top of CBVs, called *viewsets*.

Tip   For a complete list of class-based views in Django, see `ccbv.co.uk`. For the Django REST Framework, see `cdrf.co`.

CRUD Viewsets in DRF

In Chapter 1, we reviewed the concept of *resources* as one of the main building blocks of REST.

In the MVC Framework, operations on resources are handled by a controller that exposes methods for CRUD verbs. We also clarified that Django is an MVT Framework, rather than MVC. In Django and the DRF, we use class-based views to expose common CRUD operations in terms of `GET`, `POST`, `PUT`, and so on. Nevertheless, the Django REST Framework offers a clever abstraction over class-based views, called *viewsets*, which make the DRF look more "resourceful" than ever. Listing 3-1 shows a viewset, specifically a `ModelViewSet`.

Listing 3-1. A ModelViewSet in DRF

```
from rest_framework import viewsets
from .models import Blog, BlogSerializer

class BlogViewSet(viewsets.ModelViewSet):
    queryset = Blog.objects.all()
    serializer_class = BlogSerializer
```

Such a viewset gives you all the methods for handling common CRUD operations for free. Table 3-1 summarizes the relationship between viewset methods, HTTP methods, and CRUD operations.

Table 3-1. *Relationship Between Viewset Methods, HTTP Methods, and CRUD Operations*

Viewset Methods	HTTP Method	CRUD Operation
create()	POST	**C**reate resource
list() / retrieve()	GET	**R**etrieve resource(s)
update()	PUT	**U**pdate resource
destroy()	DELETE	**D**elete resource
update()	PATCH	Partial update resource

Once you have a viewset, it's only a matter of wiring up the class with an urlpatterns. Listing 3-2 shows the `urls.py` for the previous viewset.

Listing 3-2. Viewset and Urlpatterns in Django REST

```
from .views import BlogViewSet
from rest_framework.routers import DefaultRouter

router = DefaultRouter()
router.register(r"blog", BlogViewSet, basename="blog")
urlpatterns = router.urls
```

As you can see, with a minimal amount of code you have the complete collection of CRUD operations, with the corresponding URLs.

Models, Forms, and Serializers

The ability to create pages and forms with little or no code at all is what makes Django shine.

Thanks to model forms, for example, it takes a couple of lines of code to create a form starting from a Django model, complete with validation and error handling, ready to be included in a view. When you are in a hurry, you can even assemble a `CreateView`, which takes exactly three lines of code (at least) to produce the HTML form for a model, attached to the corresponding template. If Django model forms are the bridge between the end user and the database, serializers in the Django REST Framework are the bridge between the end user, our REST API, and Django models. Serializers are in charge of serialization and deserialization of Python objects, and they can be thought of as model forms for JSON. Consider the model shown in Listing 3-3.

Listing 3-3. A Django Model

```
class Quote(models.Model):
    client = models.ForeignKey(to=settings.AUTH_USER_MODEL,
    on_delete=models.CASCADE)
    proposal_text = models.TextField(blank=True)
```

From this model, we can make a DRF model serializer, shown in Listing 3-4.

Listing 3-4. A DRF Serializer

```
class QuoteSerializer(serializers.ModelSerializer):
    class Meta:
        model = Quote
        fields = ["client", "proposal_text"]
```

When we hit a DRF endpoint, the serializer converts the underlying model instances to JSON before any output is shown to the user. Vice versa, when we make a POST request against a DRF view, the serializer converts our JSON to the corresponding Python object, not before validating the input. Serializers can also express model relationships. In Listing 3-4, Quote is connected to the custom user model through a many-to-one relationship. In our serializer we can expose this relationship as an hyperlink, as shown in Listing 3-5 (remember hypermedia APIs?).

Listing 3-5. A DRF Serializer

```
class QuoteSerializer(serializers.ModelSerializer):
    client = serializers.HyperlinkedRelatedField(
        read_only=True, view_name="users-detail"
    )

    class Meta:
        model = Quote
        fields = ["client", "proposal_text"]
```

This will produce the JSON output shown in Listing 3-6.

Listing 3-6. A JSON Response with Relationships

```
[
  {
    "client": "https://api.example/api/users/1",
    "proposal_text": "Django quotation system"
  },
  {
    "client": "https://api.example/api/users/2",
    "proposal_text": "Django school management system"
  }
]
```

In Chapter 6, we use serializers to decouple our Django project. Having outlined the building blocks of the DRF, let's now explore the wonderful world of asynchronous Django.

From WSGI to ASGI

WSGI is the lingua franca of web servers to Python communication, that is, a protocol that enables the back and forth between web servers such as Gunicorn, and the underlying Python application.

As anticipated in Chapter 2, Django needs a web server to run efficiently in production. Usually, a reverse proxy such as NGINX acts as the main entry point for the end user. A Python WSGI server listens for requests behind NGINX and acts as a bridge between the HTTP request and the Django application. Everything happens synchronously in WSGI, and there was no way to rewrite the protocol without introducing breaking changes. That led the community (for this tremendous work we must thank Andrew Godwin) to write a new protocol, called ASGI, for running asynchronous Python applications under ASGI-capable web servers. To run Django asynchronously, and we are going to see what that means in the next section, we need an asynchronous-capable server. You can choose Daphne, Hypercorn, or Uvicorn. In our example, we will use Uvicorn.

Getting Started with Asynchronous Django

Asynchronous code is all about non-blocking execution. This is the magic behind platforms like Node.js, which predated the realm of high throughput services for years.

The asynchronous Python landscape instead has always been fragmented, with many PEPs and competing implementations before the arrival of `async/await` in Python 3.5 (2015). Asynchronicity in Django was a dream, until Django 3.0, when seminal support for the aforementioned ASGI found its way into the core. Asynchronous views (Django 3.1) are one of the most exciting additions to Django in recent years. To understand what problem asynchronicity solves in Django, and in Python in general, consider a simple Django view. When the user reaches this view, we fetch a list of links from an external service, as shown in Listing 3-7.

Listing 3-7. A Synchronous View Doing Network Calls

```
from django.http import JsonResponse
import httpx

client = httpx.Client(base_url="https://api.valentinog.com/demo")

def list_links(_request):
    links = client.get("/sleep/").json()
    json_response = {"links": links}
    return JsonResponse(data=json_response)
```

This should immediately raise a red flag. It can run fast, really fast, or take forever to complete, leaving the browser hanging. Due to the single-threaded nature of the Python interpreter, our code runs in sequential steps. In our view, we can't return the response to the user until the API call completes. In fact my link, `https://api.valentinog.com/demo/sleep/`, is configured to sleep for 10 seconds before returning the result. In other words, our view is blocking. Here `httpx`, the Python HTTP client I use to make requests, is configured with a safe timeout and will raise an exception after a few seconds, but not every library has this sort of security in place.

Any IO-bound operation can potentially starve resources or block the whole execution. Traditionally, to overcome this problem in Django, we would use a *task queue*, a component that runs in the background, picks up tasks to execute, and returns the result later. The most popular task queues for Django are Celery and Django Q. Task queues are highly suggested for IO-bound operations like sending emails, running scheduled jobs, HTTP requests, or for CPU-bound operations that need to run on multiple cores. Asynchronous views in Django don't completely replace task queues, especially for CPU-bound operations. Django Q for example uses Python `multiprocessing`. For non-critical IO-bound operations instead, like HTTP calls or sending emails, Django asynchronous views are great. In the most simple case, you can send out an email or call an external API without incurring the risk of blocking the user interface. So what's in an asynchronous Django view? Let's rewrite the previous example with an asynchronous view in a way that the `httpx` client retrieves data in the background; see Listing 3-8.

Listing 3-8. An Asynchronous View Doing Network Calls, This Time Safely

```
from django.http import HttpResponse
import httpx
import asyncio

async def get_links():
    base_url = "https://api.valentinog.com/demo"
    client = httpx.AsyncClient(base_url=base_url, timeout=15)
    response = await client.get("/sleep")
    json_response = response.json()
    # Do something with the response or with the json
    await client.aclose()

async def list_links(_request):
    asyncio.create_task(get_links())
    response = "<p>Fetching links in background</p>"
    return HttpResponse(response)
```

If you never worked with asynchronous Python and Django, there are a few new concepts worth clarifying in this code. First of all, we import `asyncio`, the bridge between us and the asynchronous Python world. We then declare a first asynchronous function with `async def`. In this first function, `get_links()`, we use the asynchronous `httpx` client with a timeout of 15 seconds. Since we are going to run this call in the background, we can safely increase the timeout. Next up, we use `await` in front of `client.get()`. Finally, we close the client with `client.aclose()`. To avoid leaving resources open, you can also use the asynchronous client with an asynchronous context manager. In this case, we can refactor to `async with`, as shown in Listing 3-9.

Listing 3-9. Using an Asynchronous Context Manager

```
async def get_links():
    base_url = "https://api.valentinog.com/demo"
    async with httpx.AsyncClient(base_url=base_url, timeout=15) as client:
        response = await client.get("/sleep")
        json_response = response.json()
        # Do something with the json ...
```

Tip   An asynchronous context manager is one that implements __aenter__ and __aexit__ instead of __enter__ and __exit__.

In the second asynchronous function list_links(), our Django view, we use asyncio.create_task() to run get_links() in the background. This is the real news. async def in a Django view is the most notable change from a developer's perspective. For users instead, the most evident benefit is that they don't have to wait to see the HTML if the execution takes longer than expected. In the scenario we imagined previously, for example, we can send the results to the user later with an email message. This is one of the most compelling use cases for asynchronous views in Django. But it doesn't stop here. To recap, things you can do now that asynchronous Django is a thing:

- Efficiently execute multiple HTTP requests in parallel in a view

- Schedule long-running tasks

- Interact safely with external systems

There are still things missing before Django and the DRF become 100% asynchronous—the ORM and the Django REST views are not asynchronous—but we will use asynchronous Django capabilities here and there in our decoupled project to practice.

Competing Asynchronous Frameworks and the DRF

At the time of writing, the Django REST Framework has no support for asynchronous views.

In light of this, wouldn't it be better to use something like FastAPI or Starlette for building asynchronous web services? Starlette is an ASGI framework built by Tom Christie, the DRF creator. FastAPI instead builds on top of Starlette and offers a stellar developer tooling for building asynchronous Web APIs. Both are excellent choices for greenfield projects, and luckily you don't have to choose, because FastAPI can run within Django itself, thanks to experimental projects like `django-ninja`, while we wait for asynchronous DRF.

Summary

This chapter reviewed the fundamentals of the Django REST Framework and covered how to run a simple asynchronous Django view. You learned:

- What are the DRF class-based views, viewsets, and serializers
- How to create and asynchronous Django view
- How to run Django under Uvicorn

In the next chapter, we analyze in detail the patterns for decoupling Django, while in Chapter 6, we finally get hands on with Django and JavaScript frontends.

Additional Resource

- Asynchronous Django, a playlist

CHAPTER 4

Advantages and Disadvantages of Decoupled Architectures

In this chapter, we outline various approaches for decoupling a Django project. In particular, we cover:

- Hybrid architectures
- Fully decoupled architectures based on REST and GraphQL
- Advantages and disadvantages of both styles

By the end of the chapter you should be able to discern and apply with success one or more decoupling styles to your next Django project.

Pseudo-Decoupled Django

Pseudo-decoupled, or *hybrid decoupling*, is an approach in which a static frontend is augmented with a sprinkle of JavaScript; just enough to make things interactive and playful for the end user.

In the next two sections, we go over the perks and drawbacks of a pseudo-decoupled setup by examining two different approaches: without REST and with REST.

Pseudo-Decoupled Without REST

Depending on how long you have been programming, you will begin to notice that there is a category of patterns recurring over and over when building web applications: data fetching and form handling.

© Valentino Gagliardi 2021
V. Gagliardi, *Decoupled Django*, https://doi.org/10.1007/978-1-4842-7144-5_4

For example, you might have a page for inserting new data in your Django application. How you handle data insertion is up to the user requirements, but basically you have two choices:

- Handle the form exclusively with Django

- Handle the form with JavaScript

Django forms and model forms are great with their ability to generate the fields for you, but most of the time we want to intercept the classic GET/POST/Redirect pattern of form handling, in particular the submit event of forms. To do so, we introduce a little JavaScript into the Django templates. Listing 4-1 shows such an example.

Listing 4-1. JavaScript Logic for Form Handling

```
{% block script %}
    <script>
        const form = document.getElementById("reply-create");
        form.addEventListener('submit', function (event) {

            event.preventDefault();
            const formData = new FormData(this);

            fetch("{% url "support:reply-create" %}", {
                method: 'POST',
                body: formData
            }).then(response => {
                if (!response.ok) throw Error(response.statusText);
                return response;
            }).then(() => {
                location.reload();
                window.scrollTo({top:0});
            });
        });
    });
{% endblock %}
```

In this example, we tie JavaScript to the form so that when the user submits the data, the default event for the form is intercepted and stopped. Next up we build a FormData object, which is sent to a Django CreateView. Notice also how we can use Django's url template tag to build the URL for Fetch. For this example to work, the form must have a CSRF token included, as shown in Listing 4-2.

Listing 4-2. Django's CSRF Token Template Tag

```
<form id="reply-create">
   {% csrf_token %}
   <!-- fields here -->
</form>
```

If the token is outside the form, or for any other POST request not coming directly from the form, the CSRF token must be included in the XHR request header. The example outlined here is just one of the many use cases for JavaScript into a Django template. As touched briefly in Chapter 2, we are seeing a Cambrian explosion of micro-frameworks for adding just enough interactivity to Django templates. There is not enough space to cover every possible example in this book. Here we focus on the broader architecture to examine advantages and disadvantages of each approach. Figure 4-1 shows a representation of pseudo-decoupled Django without REST.

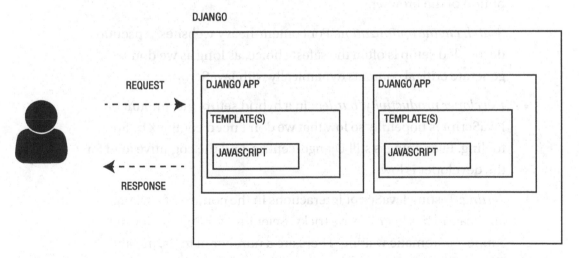

Figure 4-1. *A pseudo-decoupled Django project can have one or more apps, each with its own templates. JavaScript is blended into templates and talks to regular Django views*

Keeping in mind what Django has to offer in terms of development speed, in the case of a pseudo-decoupled, or hybrid, approach, what do we gain and what do we lose?

- *Authentication and cookies*: Since we serve JavaScript from within Django templates we don't need to worry about complex authentication methods. We can use the built-in session auth. Also, in a pseudo-decoupled setup, cookies are free to travel over each request on the same domain.

- *Forms*: Django has an amazing form system that saves tons of time during development. In a pseudo-decoupled setup, we can still use Django forms to build up the HTML structure for data insertion, with just enough JavaScript to make them interactive.

- *What JS library?* In a pseudo-decoupled setup, we can use any lightweight frontend library that doesn't require a build pipeline, such as Vue.js, or even better, vanilla JavaScript. If we know beforehand what user agent we're going to target, we can serve modern JavaScript syntax without a transpilation step.

- *Routing*: Django is in charge of routing and URL building. No need to worry about JavaScript routing libraries or weird issues with the back button of the browser.

- *Search engine optimization*: For content-heavy websites, a pseudo-decoupled setup is often the safest choice, as long as we don't generate critical contents dynamically with JavaScript.

- *Developer productivity/burden*: In a hybrid setup, the amount of JavaScript is hopefully so low that we don't need complex build tooling. Everything is still Django-centric, and the cognitive load for the developer is low.

- *Testing*: Testing JavaScript interactions in the context of a Django application has been always tricky. Selenium for Python doesn't support automatic waiting. There are a number of tools, mostly wrappers around Selenium, like Splinter, that have this capability. However, testing a pseudo-decoupled Django frontend without a JavaScript-capable test runner can be still cumbersome. Tools like Cypress, which we cover in Chapter 9, play really well with Django to ease the burden of testing JavaScript-enriched interfaces.

Pseudo-Decoupled with REST

Not every application must be architected as a single-page application, and since the beginning of this book we stressed this point.

Over-engineered applications are the root of all evil, to play along the lines of Donald Knuth. However, there are hybrid situations where the UI requires a lot of JavaScript interactivity, more than a simple form handling, but we still don't want to leave Django's umbrella. In these configurations you will find it reasonable to introduce JavaScript libraries like Vue.js or React into a Django project. While Vue.js is highly progressive, it doesn't want to take control of all the page. React forces the developer to do everything in React. In these situations the Django frontend, made out of templates and augmented with Forms or Model Forms, can lose importance in favor of a pseudo-decoupled setup, whereby:

- The frontend of one or more Django apps is built entirely with JavaScript

- The backend exposes a REST API

The difference between such a setup and an architecture where the frontend is on a different domain/origin from the REST API is that in a pseudo-decoupled setup, we serve the SPA frontend and the REST API from within the same Django project. This has a number of positive side effects. Why introduce REST in such a setup? A Django CreateView and a Model work well up to a certain point, after which we don't want to reinvent the wheel, like JSON serialization for models. Django REST paired with a modern frontend library is a solid ground for robust decoupled projects. Figure 4-2 shows a representation of pseudo-decoupled Django with REST.

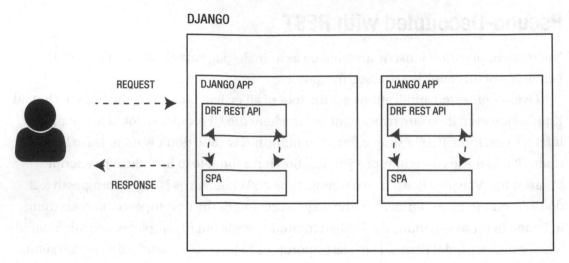

Figure 4-2. *A pseudo-decoupled Django project with REST can have one or more apps, each with its own REST API. JavaScript is served as a single-page application inside the Django project and talks to Django REST views*

In the next chapter, we see a practical example of a pseudo-decoupled setup with the Django REST Framework and Vue.js. Here, we cover advantages and disadvantages of a pseudo-decoupled configuration, as we did in the previous section for the REST-less setup.

- *Authentication and cookies*: Session-based authentication is the default choice for a pseudo-decoupled project, even with REST. Since we serve the single-page application from within the same Django project, it's only a matter of authenticating the user through a regular Django view and grabbing the appropriate cookies before making POST requests from JavaScript.

- *Forms*: If we decide to build one or more Django applications as single-page applications, we lose the ability to use Django Forms and Model Forms. This begins to lead to code duplication and more work for the team, as good 'ol Django forms and their data validation layers must be reimplemented with the JavaScript library of choice.

- *What JS library?* In a pseudo-decoupled setup with REST, we can use any JavaScript library or framework. This requires some extra steps to include the bundle in the Django static system, but it is possible with any library.

- *Routing*: Routing for single-page apps served from within a Django project is not trivial to implement. Django can still serve the main path for each single app, something like `https://decoupled-django.com/billing/` for example, but then each app must handle its internal routing. Hash-based routing is the simplest form of routing, and the easiest to implement, compared to history-based routing.

- *Search engine optimization*: Single-page applications (SPAs) are ill-suited for content-heavy websites. This is one of the most important aspects to take into account before integrating an SPA into Django.

- *Developer productivity/burden*: Any modern JavaScript library comes with its own set of challenges and tooling. In a pseudo-decoupled setup with REST and one or more single-page apps, the overhead for Python developers can increase exponentially.

- *Testing*: In a pseudo-decoupled setup with a low amount of JavaScript ,it could make sense to use tools like Selenium or Splinter, taking into account the need to implement automatic waiting for JavaScript interactions. Instead, in a pseudo-decoupled configuration based on REST and a SPA, Python-centric tools fall short. To test JavaScript-heavy interfaces and JavaScript UI components such as those implemented with Vue.js or React, tools like Cypress for functional testing and Jest for unit testing are better choices.

Fully-Decoupled Django

Opposed to a pseudo-decoupled setup, a *fully-decoupled* architecture, also called *headless*, is an approach in which the frontend and the backend are completely separated.

On the frontend we can find JavaScript single-page applications living on a different domain/origin from the backend, which now serves as a source of data with REST or GraphQL. In the next two sections, we go over both approaches.

Fully-Decoupled with REST

Fully-decoupled Django projects with REST are by far one of the most widespread setups. Thanks to its high flexibility, the REST API and the frontend may be deployed on different domains or origins. The Django REST Framework is the de-facto library for building REST APIs in Django, while JavaScript leads the frontend with React, Vue.js, and Angular. In these configurations, the architecture is usually arranged as follows:

- The frontend of one or more Django apps lives outside Django as a single-page JavaScript app

- One or more Django apps expose a REST API

A Django project configured fully-decoupled with a REST API can serve wonderfully as:

- A REST API for a SPA, a mobile app, or a Progressive Web App

- A content repository for a static site generation tool (SSG) or for a server-side rendered JavaScript project (SSR)

Figure 4-3 shows a representation of fully-decoupled Django project with REST.

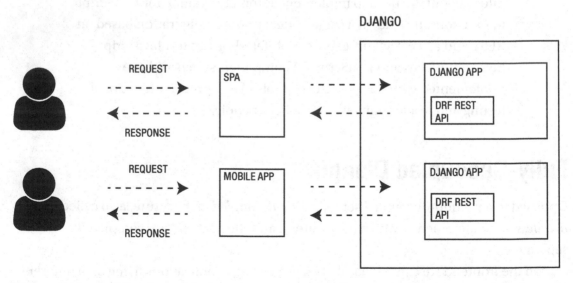

Figure 4-3. *A fully-decoupled Django project with REST can have one or more apps, each with its own REST API. JavaScript lives outside the Django project as a single-page application and talks to Django REST views through JSON*

It's important to note that not every Django app inside a project must expose a REST API: one could choose to decouple one or more facets of the application, while keeping the rest under the classic MVT arrangement. The separation of concerns prescribed by REST opens the road to flexible, but also more complex, setups. What can we expect if we decouple a Django project with REST?

- *Authentication and cookies*: Authentication for fully-decoupled projects is not trivial to implement. Session-based authentication can work with REST and single-page apps, but it breaks the stateless constraint. There are a number of different approaches to circumvent the limitations of session-based authentication for REST APIs, but in later years the community seemed oriented to embrace stateless authentication mechanisms, such as token-based authentication with JWT (JSON web tokens). However, JWT is not so welcomed in the Django community due to its security flaws and potential implementation pitfalls.

- *Forms*: Leaving Django templates and Forms means we lose the ability to build forms easily. In a fully-decoupled setup, the form layer is usually built entirely with JavaScript. Data validation often gets duplicated in the frontend, which now has to sanitize and validate the user input before sending requests to the backend.

- *What JS library?* In a fully-decoupled setup with REST, we can use any JavaScript library or framework. There isn't any particular constraint for pairing the Django REST backend with a decoupled frontend.

- *Routing:* In a fully-decoupled setup, Django does not handle routing anymore. Everything weighs on the client's shoulder. For single-page applications, one can choose to implement hash-based or history routing.

- *Search engine optimization*: Single-page applications don't play well with SEO. However, with the emergence of JavaScript static-site generators such as Gatsby, Next.js, and Nuxt.js, JavaScript developers can use the latest shiny tools to generate static pages from a headless Django project without the risk of harming SEO.

- *Developer productivity/burden*: In a fully-decoupled setup with REST and one or more single-page apps, the work for Python developers increases by orders of magnitudes. For this reason, most Django and Python web agencies have a dedicated frontend team that deals exclusively with JavaScript and its related tooling.

- *Testing*: In a fully-decoupled project, the frontend and the backend are tested separately. `APITestCase` and `APISimpleTestCase` help in testing Django REST APIs, while on the frontend we see again Jest and Cypress for testing the UI.

Fully-Decoupled with GraphQL

As with fully-decoupled Django with REST, a fully-decoupled Django project with GraphQL offers high flexibility, but also more technical challenges.

REST is a battle-tested technology. GraphQL on the other hand is pretty recent, but seems to offer some apparent advantages over REST. However, as with any new technology, developers and CTOs must assess carefully advantages and drawbacks before integrating new tools, and potentially new challenges, in production projects. Figure 4-4 shows a Django project decoupled with a GraphQL and a REST API.

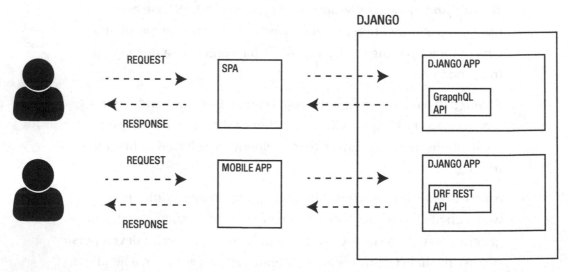

Figure 4-4. *A fully-decoupled Django project can expose REST and GraphQL APIs. It's not unusual to have both technologies in the same project*

In Figure 4-4, we imagine a fully-decoupled Django project that exposes two different apps: one with REST and another with GraphQL. In fact, GraphQL can coexist with REST to enable progressive refactorings from a legacy REST API to a GraphQL endpoint. This is useful for assessing GraphQL before switching from REST or for exposing a GraphQL API for tools like Gatsby. What is the price to pay for embracing GraphQL? Let's see.

- *Authentication and cookies*: Authentication for GraphQL in fully-decoupled setups is mostly handled with token-based authentication. On the backend, GraphQL needs to implement mutations for handling login, logout, registration, and all the related corner cases.

- *What JS library?* In a fully-decoupled setup with GraphQL, we can use any JavaScript library or framework. There isn't any particular constraint for pairing the Django GraphQL backend with a decoupled frontend. GraphQL queries can be done even with `Fetch` or `XMLHttpRequest`.

- *Search engine optimization*: GraphQL in the frontend is mostly used with client-side libraries like React. This means we cannot ship client-side generated pages as they are, or we would risk SEO damages. Tools like Gatsby, Next.js, and Nuxt.js can operate in SSG (static site generation) mode to generate static pages from a GraphQL API.

- *Developer productivity/burden*: GraphQL is a novel technology and especially in the frontend there are literally a dozen ways to implement the data fetching layer. GraphQL seems to speed up developer productivity, but at the same time it introduces new things to learn and new patterns to take into account.

Since GraphQL is a data fetching layer, considerations for forms, routing, and testing do not differ from those of a decoupled REST project.

Summary

In this chapter we outlined various approaches to decoupling a Django project:

- Pseudo-decoupled with and without REST

- Fully decoupled with REST or GraphQL

Hopefully, you are now ready to make an informed choice for your next Django project. In the next chapter, we prepare our Django project before moving to JavaScript and Vue.js.

CHAPTER 5

Setting Up a Django Project

This chapter covers:

- Setting up the Django project

In the following sections, we begin to lay down the structure of our Django project. This project will accompany us for the rest of the book. It will be expanded with a REST API in Chapter 6, and later with a GraphQL API.

Setting Up the Project

To start off, create a new folder for the project and move into it:

```
mkdir decoupled-dj && cd $_
```

Note   It is a good idea to keep the project under source control with Git. You are encouraged to initialize a repo with `git init` as soon as you create the project folder.

Once inside the folder, create a new Python virtual environment:

```
python3.9 -m venv venv
```

For the virtual environment you can use any Python version above 3; the higher the version, the better. When the environment is ready, activate it:

```
source venv/bin/activate
```

© Valentino Gagliardi 2021
V. Gagliardi, *Decoupled Django*, https://doi.org/10.1007/978-1-4842-7144-5_5

To confirm that the virtual environment is active, look for (venv) in your command prompt. If everything is in place, install Django:

```
pip install django
```

Note   It is best to install a version of Django greater than 3.1, which has support for asynchronous views.

Next up, create your Django project:

```
django-admin startproject decoupled_dj .
```

A note on the project folder structure:

- decoupled-dj is the repo root

- decoupled_dj is the actual Django project

- Django apps live in decoupled-dj

When you are ready, create two Django apps. The first app is named billing:

```
python manage.py startapp billing
```

The second app instead is a blog:

```
python manage.py startapp blog
```

A brief explanation of these apps. billing will be a Django application exposing a REST API for creating client invoices. blog will expose a REST API first, and then a GraphQL API. Now check that you have everything in place inside the project root. Run ls -1, and you should see the following output:

```
blog
billing
decoupled_dj
manage.py
venv
```

In the next section, we continue the project customization with the introduction of a custom Django user.

A Custom User

Although not strictly required for our project, a custom Django user can save you in the long run if you decide to put your project in production. Let's create one. First off, create a new app:

```
python manage.py startapp user
```

Open users/models.py and create the custom user, as shown in Listing 5-1.

Listing 5-1. A Custom Django User

```python
from django.contrib.auth.models import AbstractUser
from django.db.models import CharField

class User(AbstractUser):
    name = CharField(blank=True, max_length=100)

    def __str__(self):
        return self.email
```

We keep the custom user lean and simple with just one additional field to allow further customizations in the future. The next step would be adding AUTH_USER_MODEL to our settings file, but before doing so we need to split our settings by environment.

Tip   In the book entitled *Practical Django 2 and Channels 2* by Federico Marani (the section entitled "The User Model" in Chapter 4), you'll find another extensive example of a custom user in Django.

Interlude: Choosing the Right Database

This step has inherently nothing to do with our decoupled Django project, but using the right database is one of the most important things you can do, in any web framework. Throughout the book I will use Postgres as the database of choice. If you want to do the same, here's how to get Postgres on your machine:

- Postgres.app for MacOS

- Postgres under Docker

- Install Postgres directly on your system through a package manager

If instead you want to use SQLite, look for instructions in the next section.

Splitting the Settings File

Particularly useful when deploying in production, split settings are a way to partition Django settings depending on the environment. In a typical project, you may have:

- The *base* environment, common for all scenarios

- The *development* environment, with settings for development

- The *test* environment, with settings that apply only to testing

- The *staging* environment

- The *production* environment

The theory is that depending on the environment, Django loads its settings from a .env file. This approach is known as the *Twelve-Factor app,* first popularized by Heroku in 2011. There are many libraries for Twelve-Factor in Django. Some developers prefer to use os.environ to avoid additional dependencies altogether. My favorite library is django-environ. For our project we set up three environments: base, development, and later production. Let's install django-environ and psycopg2:

```
pip install django-environ pyscopg2-binary
```

(psycopg2 is required only if you use Postgres.) Next up, we create a new Python package named settings in decoupled_dj. Once the folder is in place, create another file for the base environment in decoupled_dj/settings/base.py. In this file, we import django-environ, and we place everything Django needs to run, regardless of the specific environment. Among these settings are:

- SECRET_KEY

- DEBUG

- INSTALLED_APPS

- MIDDLEWARE

- AUTH_USER_MODEL

Remember that in the previous section we configured a custom Django user. In the base settings we need to include the custom user app in INSTALLED_APPS, and most important, configure AUTH_USER_MODEL. Our base settings file should look like Listing 5-2.

Listing 5-2. Base Settings for Our Project

```
import environ
from pathlib import Path

BASE_DIR = Path(__file__).resolve().parent.parent
env = environ.Env()
environ.Env.read_env()
SECRET_KEY = env("SECRET_KEY")
DEBUG = env.bool("DEBUG", False)

INSTALLED_APPS = [
    "django.contrib.admin",
    "django.contrib.auth",
    "django.contrib.contenttypes",
    "django.contrib.sessions",
    "django.contrib.messages",
    "django.contrib.staticfiles",
    "users.apps.UsersConfig",
]
MIDDLEWARE = [ # OMITTED FOR BREVITY ]
ROOT_URLCONF = "decoupled_dj.urls"
TEMPLATES = [ # OMITTED FOR BREVITY ]
WSGI_APPLICATION = "decoupled_dj.wsgi.application
```

```
DATABASES = {"default": env.db()
AUTH_PASSWORD_VALIDATORS = [  # OMITTED FOR BREVITY  ]
LANGUAGE_CODE = "en-GB"
TIME_ZONE = "UTC"
USE_I18N = True
USE_L10N = True
USE_TZ = Tru
STATIC_URL = env("STATIC_URL")
AUTH_USER_MODEL = "users.User"
```

Note   I have omitted for brevity the complete code for the following configurations: MIDDLEWARE, TEMPLATES, and AUTH_PASSWORD_VALIDATORS. These should have the default values that come from stock Django.

Next up we create an .env file in the decoupled_dj/settings folder. This file will have different values depending on the environment. For development we use the values in Listing 5-3.

Listing 5-3. Environment File for Development

```
DEBUG=yes
SECRET_KEY=!changethis!
DATABASE_URL=psql://decoupleddjango:localpassword@127.0.0.1/decoupleddjango
STATIC_URL=/static/
```

If you want to use SQLite in place of Postgres, change DATABASE_URL to:

```
DATABASE_URL=sqlite:/decoupleddjango.sqlite3
```

To complete the setup, create a new file called decoupled_dj/settings/development.py and import everything from the base settings. In addition, we also customize the configuration. Here we are going to enable django-extensions, a handy library for Django in development (Listing 5-4).

Listing 5-4. decoupled_dj/settings/development.py – The Settings File for Development

```
from .base import *  # noqa
INSTALLED_APPS = INSTALLED_APPS + ["django_extensions"]
```

Let's also install the library:

```
pip install django-extensions
```

Let's not forget to export the DJANGO_SETTINGS_MODULE environment variable:

```
export DJANGO_SETTINGS_MODULE=decoupled_dj.settings.development
```

Now you can make the migrations:

```
python manage.py makemigrations
```

Finally, you can apply them to the database:

```
python manage.py migrate
```

In a moment, we will test our setup.

Bonus: Running Django Under ASGI

To run Django asynchronously, we need an ASGI server. In production, you can use Uvicorn with Gunicorn. In development, you might want to use Uvicorn standalone. Install it:

```
pip install uvicorn
```

Again, don't forget to export the DJANGO_SETTINGS_MODULE environment variable if you haven't already done so:

```
export DJANGO_SETTINGS_MODULE=decoupled_dj.settings.development
```

Next up, run the server with the following command:

```
uvicorn decoupled_dj.asgi:application
```

If everything goes well, you should see the following output:

```
INFO: Uvicorn running on http://127.0.0.1:8000 (Press CTRL+C to quit)
```

If you click on the link, you should see the familiar Django rocket! One more thing before moving forward: we need to split the requirements file.

Splitting the Requirements File

As we have done with the settings file, it is good practice to split the requirements for our Django applications. We will work in development for most of the next chapters, and for now we can split the requirements in two files: base and development. Later, we will also add dependencies for testing and production. Create a new folder called `requirements`, and place the `base.txt` and `development.txt` files into it. In the `base` file, we place the most essential dependencies for our project:

- Django

- `django-environ` for working with `.env` files

- `pyscopg2-binary` for connecting to Postgres (not required if you decided to use SQLite)

- Uvicorn for running Django under ASGI

Your `requirements/base.txt` file should look like the following:

```
Django==3.1.3
django-environ==0.4.5
psycopg2-binary==2.8.6
uvicorn==0.12.2
```

Your `requirements/development.txt` file instead should look like the following:

```
-r ./base.txt
django-extensions==3.0.9
```

Note   Your versions of these packages will most likely be different from mine by the time you read this book.

From now on, to install the dependencies of your project, you will run the following command, where the requirements file will vary depending on the environment you are in:

```
pip install -r requirements/development.txt
```

Note   It is a good moment to commit the changes you made so far and to push the work to your Git repo. You can find the source code for this chapter at `https://github.com/valentinogagliardi/decoupled-dj/tree/chapter_05_setting_up_project`.

Summary

This chapter prepared the Django project and explained how to run a Django with an asynchronous ASGI server. You learned:

- How to split settings and requirements

- How to run Django under Uvicorn

In the next chapter, we finally get hands on with Django and JavaScript frontends.

CHAPTER 6

Decoupled Django with the Django REST Framework

This chapter covers:

- The Django REST Framework with Vue.js
- Single-page applications in Django templates
- Nested DRF serializers

In this chapter, you learn how to use the Django REST Framework to expose a REST API in your Django project, and how to serve a single-page application within Django.

Building the Billing App

In the previous chapter, we created a billing app in the Django project. If you haven't done this yet, here's a quick recap. First off, configure `DJANGO_SETTINGS_MODULE`:

```
export DJANGO_SETTINGS_MODULE=decoupled_dj.settings.development
```

Then, run the `startapp` command to create the app:

```
python manage.py startapp billing
```

If you prefer more flexibility but also more typing, you can pass the settings file directly to `manage.py`:

```
python manage.py command_name --settings=decoupled_dj.settings.development
```

© Valentino Gagliardi 2021
V. Gagliardi, *Decoupled Django*, https://doi.org/10.1007/978-1-4842-7144-5_6

Here, command_name is the name of the command you want to run. You can also make a shell function out of this command to avoid typing it again and again.

Note   The rest of this chapter assumes you are in the repo root decoupled-dj, with the Python virtual environment active.

Building the Models

For this app we need a couple of Django models: Invoice for the actual invoice, and ItemLine, which represents a single row in the invoice. Let's outline the relationships between these models:

- Each Invoice can have one or many ItemLines

- An ItemLine belongs to exactly one Invoice

This is a *many-to-one* (or *one-to-many*) relationship, which means that ItemLine will have a foreign key to Invoice (if you need a refresher on this topic, check out the resources section at the end of the chapter). In addition, each Invoice is associated with a User (the custom Django user we built in Chapter 3). This means:

- A User can have many Invoices

- Each Invoice belongs to one User

To help make sense of this, Figure 6-1 shows the ER diagram on which we will build these Django models.

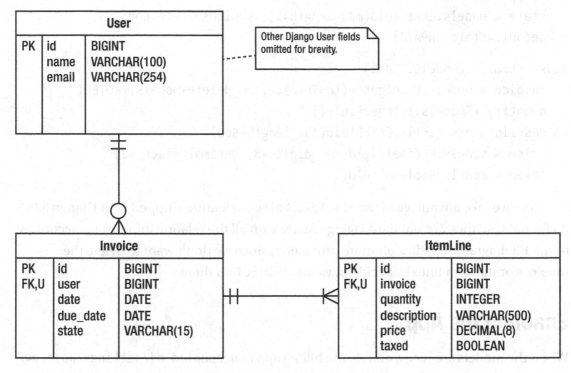

Figure 6-1. *The ER diagram for the billing application*

Having defined the entities, let's now build the appropriate Django models. Open billing/models.py and define the models as shown in Listing 6-1.

Listing 6-1. billing/models.py – The Models for the Billing App

```
from django.db import models
from django.conf import settings

class Invoice(models.Model):
    class State(models.TextChoices):
        PAID = "PAID"
        UNPAID = "UNPAID"
        CANCELLED = "CANCELLED"

    user = models.ForeignKey(to=settings.AUTH_USER_MODEL, on_delete=models.
    PROTECT)
    date = models.DateField()
    due_date = models.DateField()
```

```
    state = models.CharField(max_length=15, choices=State.choices,
    default=State.UNPAID)

class ItemLine(models.Model):
    invoice = models.ForeignKey(to=Invoice, on_delete=models.PROTECT)
    quantity = models.IntegerField()
    description = models.CharField(max_length=500)
    price = models.DecimalField(max_digits=8, decimal_places=2)
    taxed = models.BooleanField()
```

Here we take advantage of models.TextChoices, a feature shipped with Django 3.0. As for the rest, they are standard Django fields, with all the relationships set up according to the ER diagram. To add a bit more protection, since we don't want to delete the invoices or the item lines by accident, we use PROTECT on them.

Enabling the App

When the models are ready, enable the billing app in decoupled_dj/settings/base.py, as shown in Listing 6-2.

Listing 6-2. decoupled_dj/settings/base.py - Enabling the Billing App

```
INSTALLED_APPS = [
    ...
    "billing.apps.BillingConfig",
]
```

Finally, you can make and apply the migrations (these are two separate commands):

```
python manage.py makemigrations
python manage.py migrate
```

With the app in place, we are now ready to outline the interface, and later the backend code to make it work.

Wireframing the Billing App

Before talking about any frontend library, let's first see what we are going to build. Figure 6-2 shows a wireframe of the billing app, specifically, the interface for creating a new invoice.

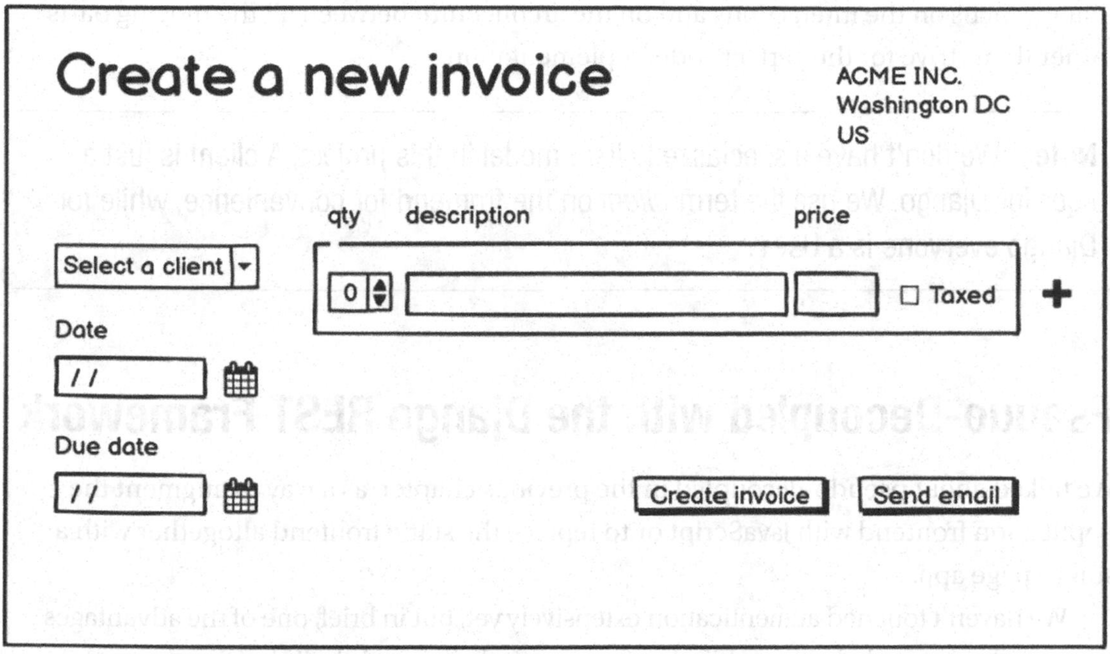

Figure 6-2. The wireframe for the billing app

Having the UI in mind before writing any code is important; this is an approach known as *outside-in* development. By looking at the interface, we can begin to think about what API endpoint we need to expose. What HTTP calls should we make from the frontend to the backend? First off, we need to fetch a list of clients to populate the `select` that says "Select a client". This is a `GET` call to an endpoint like `/billing/api/clients/`. As for the rest, it's almost all dynamic data that must be sent with a `POST` request once we compile all the fields in the invoice. This could be a request to `/billing/api/invoices/`. There is also a Send Email button, which should trigger an email. To summarize, we need to make the following calls:

- `GET` all or a subset of users from `/billing/api/clients/`

- `POST` data for a new invoice to `/billing/api/invoices/`

- `POST` for sending an email to the client (you will work on this in Chapter 11)

These interactions might sound trivial to any developer familiar with JavaScript. Nevertheless, they will help make sense of the architecture of a typical decoupled project. In the next sections, we pair a JavaScript frontend with a DRF API. Keep in mind that we focus on the interactions and on the architecture between all the moving parts rather than strive for the perfect code implementation.

Note   We don't have a specialized client model in this project. A client is just a user for Django. We use the term *client* on the frontend for convenience, while for Django everyone is a User.

Pseudo-Decoupled with the Django REST Framework

We talked about pseudo-decoupled in the previous chapter, as a way to augment the application frontend with JavaScript or to replace the static frontend altogether with a single-page app.

We haven't touched authentication extensively yet, but in brief, one of the advantages of a pseudo-decoupled approach is that we can use the fantastic built-in Django authentication, based on sessions. In the following sections, we work in practice with one of the most popular JavaScript libraries for building interactive frontends—Vue.js—to see how it fits into Django. Vue.js is a perfect match for a pseudo-decoupled Django project, thanks to its high configurability. If you are wondering, we will cover React later in the book.

Vue.js and Django

Let's start off with Vue. We want to serve our single-page application from within a Django template.

To do so, we must set up a Vue project. First off, install Vue CLI:

```
npm install -g @vue/cli
```

Now we need to create the Vue project somewhere. Vue is highly configurable; in most cases it's up to you to decide where to put the app. To keep things consistent we create the Vue app inside the billing folder, where our Django app already lives. Move inside the folder and run Vue CLI:

```
cd billing
vue create vue_spa
```

The installer will ask whether we want to manually select the features or use the default preset. For our project, we pick the following configurations:

- Vue 2.x

- Babel

- No routing

- Linter/formatter (ESLint and Prettier)

- Configuration in dedicated config files

Press Enter and let the installer configure the project. When the package manager finishes pulling in all the dependencies, take a minute to explore the Vue project structure. Once you're done, you are ready to explore all the steps for making the single-page app work within Django.

To keep things manageable, we target only the development environment for now (we cover production in the next chapter). As anticipated in Chapter 2, Django can serve static files in development with the integrated server. When we run `python manage.py runserver`, Django collects all the static assets, as long as we configure `STATIC_URL`. In Chapter 3, we split all the settings for our project, and we configured `STATIC_URL` as `/static/` for development. Out of the box, Django can collect static files from each app folder, and for our billing app, this means we need to put static assets in `billing/static`.

With a bunch of simple JavaScript files this is easy. You simply place them in the appropriate folder. With a CLI tool like Vue CLI or create-react-app instead, the destination folder for the JavaScript bundle and for all other static assets is already decided for you by the tool. For Vue CLI, this folder is named `dist`, and it is meant to end up in the same project folder of your single-page app. This is bad for Django, which won't be able to pick up these static files. Luckily, thanks to Vue's configurability, we can put our JavaScript build and the template where Django expects them. We can decide where static files and `index.html` should end up through `vue.config.js`. Since Vue CLI has an integrated development server with hot reloading, we have two options at this point in development:

- We serve the app with `npm run serve`

- We serve the app through Django's development server

With the first option, we can run and access the app at `http://localhost:8081/` to see changes in real time. With the second option, is convenient to get a more real-world feeling: for example we can use the built-in authentication system. In order to go with the second option, we need to configure Vue CLI.

To start off, in the Vue project folder `billing/vue_spa`, create an environment file named `.env.staging` with the following content:

```
VUE_APP_STATIC_URL=/static/billing/
```

Note that this is the combination between Django's `STATIC_URL`, which we aptly configured in `decoupled_dj/settings/.env`, and Django's app folder called `billing`. Next up, create `vue.config.js` in the same Vue project folder, with the content shown in Listing 6-3.

Listing 6-3. billing/vue_spa/vue.config.js – Vue's Custom Configuration

```
const path = require("path");

module.exports = {
 publicPath: process.env.VUE_APP_STATIC_URL,
 outputDir: path.resolve(__dirname, "../static", "billing"),
 indexPath: path.resolve(__dirname, "../templates/", "billing",
 "index.html")
};
```

With this configuration, we tell Vue to:

- Use the path specified at `.env.staging` as the `publicPath`

- Put static assets to `outputDir` inside `billing/static/billing`

- Put the `index.html` to `indexPath` inside `billing/templates/billing`

This setup respects Django expectations about where to find static files and the main template. `publicPath` is the path at which the Vue app is expecting to be deployed. In development/staging, we can point to `/static/billing/`, where Django will serve the files. In production, we provide a different path.

Note   Django is highly configurable in regard to static files and template structure. You are free to experiment with alternative setups. Throughout the book we will adhere to the stock Django structure.

Now you can build your Vue project in "staging" mode (you should run this command from the Vue project folder):

```
npm run build -- --mode staging
```

After running the build, you should see Vue files landing in the expected folders:

- Static assets go in `billing/static/billing`

- `index.html` goes in `billing/templates/billing`

To test things out, we need to wire up a view and the URLs in Django. First off, in `billing/views.py` create a subclass of `TemplateView` to serve Vue's `index.html`, as shown in Listing 6-4.

Listing 6-4. billing/views.py - Template View for Serving the App Entry Point

```
from django.views.generic import TemplateView

class Index(TemplateView):
    template_name = "billing/index.html"
```

Note   If you like function view more, you can use the `render()` shortcut with a function view instead of a `TemplateView`.

Next up, configure the main route in `billing/urls.py`, as shown in Listing 6-5.

Listing 6-5. billing/urls.py - URL Configuration

```
from django.urls import path
from .views import Index

app_name = "billing"
```

```
urlpatterns = [
    path("", Index.as_view(), name="index")
]
```

Finally, include the URL for the billing app in decoupled_dj/urls.py, as shown in Listing 6-6.

Listing 6-6. decoupled_dj/urls.py - Project URL Configuration

```
from django.urls import path, include

urlpatterns = [
    path(
        "billing/",
        include("billing.urls", namespace="billing")
    ),
]
```

You can now run Django development server in another terminal:

```
python manage.py runserver
```

If you visit http://127.0.0.1:8000/billing/, you should see your Vue app up and running, as shown in Figure 6-3.

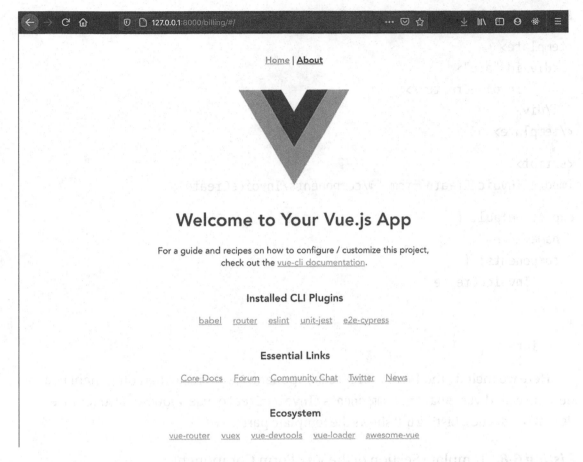

Figure 6-3. *Our Vue app is served by Django's development server*

You may wonder why we use the term *staging*, and not *development,* for this setup. What you get out of this configuration, really, is more like a "pre-staging" environment where you can test the Vue app within Django. The drawback of this configuration is that to see changes reflected, we need to rebuild the Vue app every time. Of course nothing stops you from running `npm run serve` to start the Vue app with the integrated webpack server. In the next sections, we complete the UI for our billing app, and finally the REST backend.

Building the Vue App

Let's now build our Vue app. To start off, wipe the boilerplate from `vue_spa/src/App.vue` and start with the code shown in Listing 6-7.

Listing 6-7. Main Vue Component

```
<template>
  <div id="app">
      <InvoiceCreate />
  </div>
</template>

<script>
import InvoiceCreate from "@/components/InvoiceCreate";

export default {
  name: "App",
  components: {
      InvoiceCreate
  }
};
</script>
```

Here we include the InvoiceCreate component. Now, create this component in a new file called vue_spa/src/components/InvoiceCreate.vue, (you can also remove HelloWorld.vue). Listing 6-8 shows the template part first.

Listing 6-8. Template Section of the Vue Form Component

```
<template>
 <div class="container">
   <h2>Create a new invoice</h2>
   <form @submit.prevent="handleSubmit">
     <div class="form">
       <div class="form__aside">
         <div class="form__field">
           <label for="user">Select a client</label>
           <select id="user" name="user" required>
             <option value="--">--</option>
             <option v-for="user in users" :key="user.email" :value="user.id">
               {{ user.name }} - {{ user.email }}
             </option>
```

```
      </select>
    </div>
    <div class="form__field">
      <label for="date">Date</label>
      <input id="date" name="date" type="date" required />
    </div>
    <div class="form__field">
      <label for="due_date">Due date</label>
      <input id="due_date" name="due_date" type="date" required />
    </div>
  </div>
  <div class="form__main">
    <div class="form__field">
      <label for="quantity">Qty</label>
      <input
        id="quantity"
        name="quantity"
        type="number"
        min="0"
        max="10"
        required
      />
    </div>
    <div class="form__field">
      <label for="description">Description</label>
      <input id="description" name="description" type="text" required />
    </div>
    <div class="form__field">
      <label for="price">Price</label>
      <input
        id="price"
        name="price"
        type="number"
        min="0"
```

```
            step="0.01"
            required
          />
        </div>
        <div class="form__field">
          <label for="taxed">Taxed</label>
          <input id="taxed" name="taxed" type="checkbox" />
        </div>
      </div>
    </div>
    <div class="form__buttons">
      <button type="submit">Create invoice</button>
      <button disabled>Send email</button>
    </div>
  </form>
 </div>
</template>
```

In this markup we have:

- The select for choosing the client

- Two date inputs

- Inputs for quantity, description, and price

- A checkbox for taxed

- Two buttons

Next up we have the logic part, with the quintessential form handling, as shown in Listing 6-9.

Listing 6-9. JavaScript Section of the Vue Form Component

```
<script>
export default {
 name: "InvoiceCreate",
 data: function() {
   return {
```

```
    users: [
      { id: 1, name: "xadrg", email: "xadrg@acme.io" },
      { id: 2, name: "olcmf", email: "olcmf@zyx.dev" }
    ]
  };
},
methods: {
  handleSubmit: function(event) {
    // eslint-disable-next-line no-unused-vars
    const formData = new FormData(event.target);

    // TODO - build the request body
    const data = {};

    fetch("/billing/api/invoices/", {
      method: "POST",
      headers: { "Content-Type": "application/json" },
      body: JSON.stringify(data)
    })
      .then(response => {
        if (!response.ok) throw Error(response.statusText);
        return response.json();
      })
      .then(json => {
        console.log(json);
      })
      .catch(err => console.log(err));
  }
},
mounted() {
  fetch("/billing/api/clients/")
    .then(response => {
      if (!response.ok) throw Error(response.statusText);
      return response.json();
    })
    .then(json => {
```

```
        this.users = json;
    });
  }
};
</script>
```

In this code we have:

- A `users` property inside the Vue component state

- A method for handling the form submit

- A `mounted` lifecycle method for fetching data on mount

Also, we target our API endpoints (not yet implemented): `/billing/api/clients/` and `/billing/api/invoices/`. You can notice some fake data in `users`; this is so we have a minimal usable interface while we wait for building the REST API.

Tip   You can develop the frontend without a backend, with tools like Mirage JS, which can intercept and respond to HTTP calls.

To make the code work, remember to put the template and the script part in order in `vue_spa/src/components/InvoiceCreate.vue`. With this minimal implementation, you are now ready to start the project in two ways. To build the app and serve it with Django, run the following in the Vue project folder:

```
npm run build -- --mode staging
```

Then, start the Django development server and head over to `http://localhost:8000/billing/`. To run Vue with its development server instead, run the following inside the Vue folder:

```
npm run serve
```

The app will start at `http://localhost:8081/`, but since we don't have the backend yet, nothing will work for the end user. In the meantime, we can set up the application so that:

- When launched under Django's umbrella, it calls `/billing/api/clients/` and `/billing/api/invoices/`

- When called with the integrated webpack server, it calls
  `http://localhost:8000/billing/api/clients/` and `http://localhost:8000/billing/api/invoices/`, which are the endpoints
  where the DRF will listen

To do this, open `vue.config.js` and add the lines in Listing 6-10 in the
configuration.

Listing 6-10. Development Server Configuration for Vue CLI

```
// omitted
module.exports = {
  // omitted
  devServer: {
      proxy: "http://localhost:8000"
  }
};
```

This ensures the project works well in staging/production with a pseudo-decoupled
setup, and in development as a standalone app. In a minute, we will finally build the
REST backend.

Vue.js, Django, and CSS

At this point you may wonder where CSS fits into the big picture. Our Vue component
does have some classes, but we didn't show any CSS pipeline in the previous section.

The reason is that there are at least two approaches for working with CSS in a project
like the one we are building. Specifically, you can:

- Include CSS in a base Django template

- Include CSS from each single-page app

At the time of this writing, Tailwind is one of the most popular CSS libraries on the
Django scene. In a pseudo-decoupled setup, you can configure Tailwind in the main
Django project, include the CSS bundle in a base template, and have a single-page Vue
app extend the base template. If each single-page app is independent, each one with
its own style, you can configure Tailwind and friends individually. Be aware that the
maintainability of the second approach might be a bit difficult in the long run.

Note You can find a minimal CSS implementation for the component in the source code for this chapter at `https://github.com/valentinogagliardi/` `decoupled-dj/tree/chapter_06_decoupled_with_drf`.

Building the REST Backend

We left a note in our Vue component that says `// TODO - build the request body`. This is because with the form we built, we cannot send the request as it is to the Django REST Framework. You'll see the reason in a moment. In the meantime, with the UI in place, we can wire up the backend with the DRF. Based on the endpoints we call from the UI, we need to expose the following sources:

- `/billing/api/clients/`

- `/billing/api/invoices/`

Let's also recap the relationships between all the entities:

- Each `Invoice` can have one or many `ItemLines`

- An `ItemLine` belongs to exactly one `Invoice`

- A `User` can have many `Invoices`

- Each `Invoice` belongs to one `User`

What does this mean? When POSTing to the backend to create a new invoice, Django wants:

- The user ID to associate the invoice with

- One or more item lines to associate the invoice with

The user is not a problem because we grab it from the first API call to `/billing/` `api/clients/`. Each item and the associated invoice cannot be sent as a whole from the frontend. We need to:

- Build the correct object in the frontend

- Adjust the ORM logic in the DRF to save related objects

Building the Serializers

To start off, we need to create the following components in the DRF:

- A serializer for User

- A serializer for Invoice

- A serializer for ItemLine

As a first step let's install the Django REST Framework:

```
pip install djangorestframework
```

Once it's installed, update requirements/base.txt to include the DRF:

```
Django==3.1.3
django-environ==0.4.5
psycopg2-binary==2.8.6
uvicorn==0.12.2
djangorestframework==3.12.2
```

Next up, enable the DRF in decoupled_dj/settings/base.py, as shown in Listing 6-11.

Listing 6-11. decoupled_dj/settings/base.py - Django Installed Apps with the DRF Enabled

```
INSTALLED_APPS = [
    ...
    "users.apps.UsersConfig",
    "billing.apps.BillingConfig",
    "rest_framework", # enables DRF
]
```

Now create a new Python package named api in billing so that we have a billing/api folder. In this package, we place all the logic for our REST API. Let's now build the serializers. Create a new file called billing/api/serializers.py with the content shown in Listing 6-12.

Listing 6-12. billing/api/serializers.py – The DRF Serializers

```python
from users.models import User
from billing.models import Invoice, ItemLine
from rest_framework import serializers

class UserSerializer(serializers.ModelSerializer):
    class Meta:
        model = User
        fields = ["id", "name", "email"]

class ItemLineSerializer(serializers.ModelSerializer):
    class Meta:
        model = ItemLine
        fields = ["quantity", "description", "price", "taxed"]

class InvoiceSerializer(serializers.ModelSerializer):
    items = ItemLineSerializer(many=True, read_only=True)

    class Meta:
        model = Invoice
        fields = ["user", "date", "due_date", "items"]
```

Here we have three serializers. UserSerializer will serialize our User model. ItemLineSerializer is the serializer for an ItemLine. Finally, InvoiceSerializer will serialize our Invoice model. Each serializer subclasses the DRF's ModelSerializer, which we encountered in Chapter 3, and has the appropriate fields mapping to the corresponding model. The last serializer in the list, InvoiceSerializer, is interesting because it contains a nested ItemLineSerializer. It's this serializer that needs some work to comply with our frontend. To see why, let's build the views.

Building the Views and the URL

Create a new file called billing/api/views.py with the code shown in Listing 6-13.

Listing 6-13. billing/api/views.py - DRF Views

```python
from .serializers import InvoiceSerializer, UserSerializer, User
from rest_framework.generics import CreateAPIView, ListAPIView
```

```python
class ClientList(ListAPIView):
    serializer_class = UserSerializer
    queryset = User.objects.all()

class InvoiceCreate(CreateAPIView):
    serializer_class = InvoiceSerializer
```

These views will respond respectively to /billing/api/clients/ and /billing/api/invoices/. Here, ClientList is a subclass of the generic DRF list view. InvoiceCreate instead subclasses the DRF's generic create view. We are now ready to wire up the URLs for our app. Open billing/urls.py and define your routes as shown in Listing 6-14.

Listing 6-14. billing/urls.py - URL Patterns for the Billing API

```python
from django.urls import path
from .views import Index
from .api.views import ClientList, InvoiceCreate

app_name = "billing"

urlpatterns = [
    path("", Index.as_view(), name="index"),
    path(
        "api/clients/",
        ClientList.as_view(),
        name="client-list"),
    path(
        "api/invoices/",
        InvoiceCreate.as_view(),
        name="invoice-create"),
]
```

Here, app_name paired with a namespace in the main project URL will allow us to call billing:client-list and billing:invoice-create with reverse(), which is particularly useful in testing. As a last step, you should have the URLs configured in decoupled_dj/urls.py, as shown in Listing 6-15.

Listing 6-15. decoupled_dj/urls.py - The Main Project URL Configuration

```python
from django.urls import path, include

urlpatterns = [
    path(
        "billing/",
        include("billing.urls", namespace="billing")
    ),
]
```

We are ready to test things out. To create a couple of models in the database, you can launch an enhanced shell (this comes from `django-extensions`):

```
python manage.py shell_plus
```

To create the models, run the following queries (>>> is the shell prompt):

```
>>> User.objects.create_user(username="jul81", name="Juliana",
email="juliana@acme.io")
>>> User.objects.create_user(username="john89", name="John", email="john@
zyx.dev")
```

Exit the shell and start Django:

```
python manage.py runserver
```

In another terminal, run the following `curl` command and see what happens:

```
curl -X POST --location "http://127.0.0.1:8000/billing/api/invoices/" \
    -H "Accept: */*" \
    -H "Content-Type: application/json" \
    -d "{
        \"user\": 1,
        \"date\": \"2020-12-01\",
        \"due_date\": \"2020-12-30\"
    }"
```

As a response you should see the following output:

```
{"user":1,"date":"2020-12-01","due_date":"2020-12-30"}
```

This is the Django REST Framework telling us it created a new invoice in the database. So far so good. How about adding some items to the invoice now? To do so, we need to make the serializer writable. In `billing/api/serializers.py`, remove `read_only=True` from the field `items` so that it looks like Listing 6-16.

Listing 6-16. billing/api/serializers.py - The Serializer for an Invoice, Now with a Writable Relationship

```
class InvoiceSerializer(serializers.ModelSerializer):
    items = ItemLineSerializer(many=True)

    class Meta:
        model = Invoice
        fields = ["user", "date", "due_date", "items"]
```

You can test again with curl, this time by passing also two items:

```
curl -X POST --location "http://127.0.0.1:8000/billing/api/invoices/" \
    -H "Accept: application/json" \
    -H "Content-Type: application/json" \
    -d "{
        \"user\": 1,
        \"date\": \"2020-12-01\",
        \"due_date\": \"2020-12-30\",
        \"items\": [
          {
            \"quantity\": 2,
            \"description\": \"JS consulting\",
            \"price\": 9800.00,
            \"taxed\": false
          },
          {
            \"quantity\": 1,
            \"description\": \"Backend consulting\",
            \"price\": 12000.00,
            \"taxed\": true
          }
        ]
      }"
```

At this point everything should blow up, and you should see the following exception:

```
TypeError: Invoice() got an unexpected keyword argument 'items'
Exception Value: Got a TypeError when calling Invoice.objects.create().
```

This may be because you have a writable field on the serializer class that is not a valid argument to Invoice.objects.create(). You may need to make the field read-only or override the InvoiceSerializer.create() method to handle this correctly.

Django REST is asking us to tweak create() in InvoiceSerializer so it can accept items alongside with the invoice.

Working with Nested Serializers

Open billing/api/serializers.py and modify the serializer as shown in Listing 6-17.

Listing 6-17. billing/api/serializers.py - The Serializer for an Invoice, Now with a Customized create()

```python
class InvoiceSerializer(serializers.ModelSerializer):
    items = ItemLineSerializer(many=True)

    class Meta:
        model = Invoice
        fields = ["user", "date", "due_date", "items"]

    def create(self, validated_data):
        items = validated_data.pop("items")
        invoice = Invoice.objects.create(**validated_data)
        for item in items:
            ItemLine.objects.create(invoice=invoice, **item)
        return invoice
```

This is also a good moment to tweak the ItemLine model. As you can see from the serializer, we are using the items field to set related items on a given invoice. The problem is, there is no such field available in the Invoice model. This is because reverse relationships on a Django model are accessible as *modelname*_set unless configured differently. To fix the field, open billing/models.py and add the related_name attribute to the invoice row, as shown in Listing 6-18.

Listing 6-18. billing/models.py - The ItemLine Model with a related_name

```python
class ItemLine(models.Model):
    invoice = models.ForeignKey(
        to=Invoice, on_delete=models.PROTECT, related_name="items"
    )
    ...
```

After saving the file, run the migration as follows:

```
python manage.py makemigrations billing
python manage.py migrate
```

After starting Django, you should now be able to repeat the same curl request, this time with success. At this stage, we can fix the frontend as well.

Fixing the Vue Frontend

In vue_spa/src/components/InvoiceCreate.vue, locate the line that says
// TODO - build the request body and adjust the code as shown in Listing 6-19.

Listing 6-19. The handleSubmit Method from the Vue Component

```javascript
methods: {
  handleSubmit: function(event) {
    const formData = new FormData(event.target);

    const data = Object.fromEntries(formData);
    data.items = [
      {
        quantity: formData.get("quantity"),
        description: formData.get("description"),
        price: formData.get("price"),
        taxed: Boolean(formData.get("taxed"))
      }
    ];
```

```
  fetch("/billing/api/invoices/", {
    method: "POST",
    headers: { "Content-Type": "application/json" },
    body: JSON.stringify(data)
  })
    // omitted;
  }
}
```

For brevity, I show only the relevant portion. Here, we use `Object.fromEntries()` (ECMAScript 2019) to build an object from our form. We then proceed to add an array of items (it has just one item for now) to the object. We finally send the object as the body payload for `fetch`. You can run Vue with the integrated server (from within the Vue project folder):

```
npm run serve
```

You should see a form that creates an invoice at `http://localhost:8080/`. Try to fill the form and click on Create Invoice. In the browser console, you should see the response from the Django REST Framework, with the invoice being successfully saved to the database. Great job! We finished the first real feature of this decoupled Django project.

Note   It is a good moment to commit the changes you made so far and to push the work to your Git repo. You can find the source code for this chapter at `https://github.com/valentinogagliardi/decoupled-dj/tree/chapter_06_decoupled_with_drf`.

┌───┐
│ **EXERCISE 6-1: HANDLING MULTIPLE ITEMS** │
└───┘

Extend the Vue component to handle multiple items for the invoice. The user should be able to click on a plus (+) button to add more items to the form, which should be sent along with the request.

Summary

This chapter paired up a Vue.js frontend with a Django REST Framework API, with Vue.js served in the same context as the main Django project.

By doing so, you learned how to:

- Integrate Vue.js into Django

- Interact with a DRF API from JavaScript

- Work with nested serializers in the Django REST Framework

In the next chapter, we approach a more real-world scenario. We discuss security and deployment, before moving again to the JavaScript land, with Next.js in Chapter 8.

Additional Resource

- Understanding many-to-one in Django

CHAPTER 7

API Security and Deployment

This chapter covers:

- Django hardening

- REST API hardening

- Deployment to production

In the previous chapter, we assembled a pseudo-decoupled Django project with the Django REST Framework and Vue.js.

It's now time to explore the security implications of such a setup, which are not so dissimilar from running a monolith, but do require some extra steps due to the presence of the REST API. After a focus on security, in the second part of the chapter we cover deployment to production with Gunicorn and NGINX.

Note In the first part of this chapter, we assume you are in the repo root decoupled-dj, with the Python virtual environment active, and with DJANGO_SETTINGS_MODULE configured as decoupled_dj.settings. development.

Django Hardening

Django is one of the most secure web frameworks out there.

However, it's easy to let things slip out, especially when we are in a hurry to see our project up and running in production. Before exposing our website or our API to the world, we need to take care of some extra details to avoid surprises. It's important to keep

© Valentino Gagliardi 2021
V. Gagliardi, *Decoupled Django*, https://doi.org/10.1007/978-1-4842-7144-5_7

in mind that the suggestions provided in this chapter are far from exhaustive. Security is a huge topic, not counting that each project and each team might have different needs when it comes to security, due to regional regulations or governmental requirements.

Django Settings for Production

In Chapter 5, in the "Splitting the Settings File" section, we configured our Django project to use different settings for each environment.

As of now, we have the following settings:

- `decoupled_dj/settings/base.py`

- `decoupled_dj/settings/development.py`

To prepare the project for production, we create another settings file in `decoupled_dj/settings/production.py`, which will hold all the production-related settings. What should go in this file? Some of the most important settings for production in Django are:

- `SECURE_SSL_REDIRECT`: Ensures that every request via HTTP gets redirected to HTTPS

- `ALLOWED_HOSTS`: Drives what hostnames Django will serve

- `STATIC_ROOT`: Is where Django will look for static files

In addition to these settings, there are also DRF-related configurations, which we touch on in the next sections. There are also a lot more authentication-related settings that we cover in Chapter 10. To start off, create `decoupled_dj/settings/production.py` and configure it as shown in Listing 7-1.

Listing 7-1. decoupled_dj/settings/production.py – The First Settings for Production

```
from .base import *  # noqa

SECURE_SSL_REDIRECT = True
ALLOWED_HOSTS = env.list("ALLOWED_HOSTS")
STATIC_ROOT = env("STATIC_ROOT")
```

These settings will be read from an `.env` file, depending on the environment. In development, we have the settings shown in Listing 7-2.

Listing 7-2. The Development .env File

```
DEBUG=yes
SECRET_KEY=!changethis!
DATABASE_URL=psql://decoupleddjango:localpassword@127.0.0.1/decoupleddjango
STATIC_URL=/static/
```

Note   How does DEBUG work here if we pass yes instead of a Boolean? The conversion is handled by django-environ for us.

In production, we need to tweak this file according to the requirements we describe in decoupled_dj/settings/production.py. This means we must deploy the .env file shown in Listing 7-3.

Listing 7-3. decoupled_dj/settings/.env.production.example - The Production .env File

```
ALLOWED_HOSTS=decoupled-django.com,static.decoupled-django.com
DEBUG=no
SECRET_KEY=!changethis!
DATABASE_URL=psql://decoupleddjango:localpassword@127.0.0.1/decoupleddjango
STATIC_URL=https://static.decoupled-django.com
STATIC_ROOT=static/
```

Note   The database settings shown here assume we are using Postgres as the database for the project. To use SQLite instead, change the database configuration to DATABASE_URL=sqlite:/decoupleddjango.sqlite3.

It is of utmost importance in production to disable DEBUG to avoid error leaking. In the previous file, note how the static related settings are slightly different from development:

- STATIC_URL is now configured to read static assets from a static. decoupled-django.com subdomain

- STATIC_ROOT in production will read files from the static folder

With this basic configuration for production, we can move to harden our Django project a little bit more, with authentication.

Authentication and Cookies in Django

In the previous chapter, we configured a Vue.js single-page app, served from a Django view. Let's review the code in `billing/views.py`, which is summarized in Listing 7-4.

Listing 7-4. billing/views.py - A TemplateView Serves the Vue.js SPA

```
from django.views.generic import TemplateView

class Index(TemplateView):
    template_name = "billing/index.html"
```

Locally, we can access the view at `http://127.0.0.1:8000/billing/` after running the Django development server, which is fine. However, once the project goes live, nothing stops anonymous users from freely reaching the view and making unauthenticated requests. To harden our project, we can, first of all, require authentication on the view with the `LoginRequiredMixin` for class-based views. Open `billing/views.py` and change the view, as shown in Listing 7-5.

Listing 7-5. billing/views.py - Adding Authentication to the Billing View

```
from django.contrib.auth.mixins import LoginRequiredMixin
from django.views.generic import TemplateView

class Index(LoginRequiredMixin, TemplateView):
    template_name = "billing/index.html"
```

From now on, any user who wants to access this view must authenticate. For us at this stage, it's enough to create a superuser in development with the following command:

```
python manage.py createsuperuser
```

Once this is done, we can authenticate through the admin view, and then visit `http://127.0.0.1:8000/billing/` to create new invoices. But as soon as we fill the form and click on Create Invoice, Django will return an error. In the Network tab of the browser's console, after trying to submit the form, we should see the following error in the response from the server:

```
"CSRF Failed: CSRF token missing or incorrect."
```

Django has a protection against CSRF attacks, and it won't let us submit AJAX requests without a valid CSRF token. In traditional Django forms, this token is usually included as a template tag, and it's sent to the backend by the browser as a cookie. However, when the frontend is built entirely with JavaScript, the CSRF token must be retrieved from the cookie storage and sent alongside the request as a header. To fix this problem in our Vue.js app, we can use vue-cookies, a convenient library for handling cookies. In a terminal, move to the Vue project folder called billing/vue_spa and run the following command:

```
npm i vue-cookies
```

Next up, load the library in billing/vue_spa/src/main.js, as shown in Listing 7-6.

Listing 7-6. billing/vue_spa/src/main.js - Enabling Vue-Cookies

```
...
import VueCookies from "vue-cookies";
Vue.use(VueCookies);
...
```

Finally, in billing/vue_spa/src/components/InvoiceCreate.vue, grab the cookie and include it as a header, as outlined in Listing 7-7.

Listing 7-7. billing/vue_spa/src/components/InvoiceCreate.vue - Including the CSRF Token in the AJAX Request

```
...
    const csrfToken = this.$cookies.get("csrftoken");

    fetch("/billing/api/invoices/", {
      method: "POST",
      headers: {
        "Content-Type": "application/json",
        "X-CSRFToken": csrfToken
      },
```

```
    body: JSON.stringify(data)
  })
    .then(response => {
      if (!response.ok) throw Error(response.statusText);
      return response.json();
    })
    .then(json => {
      console.log(json);
    })
    .catch(err => console.log(err));
...
```

To test things out, we can rebuild the Vue app with the following command:

```
npm run build -- --mode staging
```

After running Django, the creation of a new invoice at `http://127.0.0.1:8000/billing/` should now work as expected.

Note   A popular alternative to Fetch, axios can help with an interceptor feature. It's convenient for attaching cookies or other headers globally, on each request.

Back to the authentication front. At this stage, we enabled the most straightforward authentication method in Django: session-based authentication. This is one of the most traditional and most robust authentication mechanisms in Django. It relies on sessions, saved in the Django database. When the user logs in with credentials, Django stores a session in the database and sends back two cookies to the user's browser: `csrftoken` and `sessionid`. When the user makes requests to the website, the browser sends back these cookies, which Django validates against what has been stored in the database. Since HTTPS encryption is a mandatory requirement for websites these days, it makes sense to disable the transmission of `csrftoken` and `sessionid` over plain HTTP. To do so, we can add two configuration directives in `decoupled_dj/settings/production.py`, as shown in Listing 7-8.

Listing 7-8. decoupled_dj/settings/production.py - Securing Authentication Cookies

```
...
CSRF_COOKIE_SECURE = True
SESSION_COOKIE_SECURE = True
...
```

With CSRF_COOKIE_SECURE and SESSION_COOKIE_SECURE set to True, we ensure that session authentication related cookies are transmitted only over HTTPS.

Randomize the Admin URL

The built-in admin panel is probably one of the most beloved Django features. However, the URL for this panel, which by default is admin/, can be targeted by automated brute force attacks when the website is exposed online. To mitigate the issue, we can introduce a bit of randomness in the URL, by changing it to something not easily guessable. This change needs to happen in the project root decoupled_dj/urls.py, as shown in Listing 7-9.

Listing 7-9. decoupled_dj/urls.py - Hiding the Real Admin URL in Production

```
from django.urls import path, include
from django.contrib import admin
from django.conf import settings

urlpatterns = [
    path("billing/", include("billing.urls", namespace="billing")),
]

if settings.DEBUG:
    urlpatterns = [
        path("admin/", admin.site.urls),
    ] + urlpatterns

if not settings.DEBUG:
    urlpatterns = [
        path("77randomAdmin@33/", admin.site.urls),
    ] + urlpatterns
```

This code tells Django to change the admin URL from `admin/` to `77randomAdmin@33/` when `DEBUG` is `False`. With this little change, we add a bit more protection to the admin panel. Let's now see what we can do to improve the security of our REST API.

REST API Hardening

What is better than a REST API? A secure REST API, of course.

In the following sections, we will cover a set of strategies for improving the security posture of our REST API. To do so, we borrow some guidance from the REST Security Cheat Sheet by the OWASP foundation.

HTTPS Encryption and HSTS

HTTPS is a must for every website these days.

By configuring `SECURE_SSL_REDIRECT` in our Django project, we ensure that our REST API is secured as well. When we cover deployment in the next sections, we will see that in our setup, NGINX provides SSL termination for our Django project. In addition to HTTPS, we can also configure Django to attach an HTTP header named `Strict-Transport-Security` to the response. By doing so, we ensure that browsers will connect to our websites only through HTTPS. This feature is called HSTS, and while Django has HSTS-related settings, it is common practice to add these headers at the webserver/proxy level. The website `https://securityheaders.com` offers a free scanner that can help in identifying what security headers can be added to the NGINX configuration.

Audit Logging

Audit logging refers to the practice of writing logs for each action carried in a system—be it a web application, a REST API, or a database—as a way to record "who did what" at a particular point in time.

Paired with a log aggregation system, audit logging is a great way to improve data security. The OWASP REST Security Cheat Sheet prescribes audit logging for REST APIs. Out of the box, Django already provides some minimal form of audit logging in the admin. Also, the user table in Django records the last login of each user in the system. But these two trails are far from being a full-fledged audit logging solution and do not cover the REST API. There are a couple of packages for Django to add audit logging capabilities:

- `django-simple-history`
- `django-auditlog`

`django-simple-history` can track changes on models. This capability, paired with access logging, can provide effective audit logging for Django projects. `django-simple-history` is a mature package, actively supported. On the other hand, `django-auditlog` provides the same functionalities, but it is still in development at the time of this writing.

Cross-Origin Resource Sharing

In a decoupled setup, JavaScript is the main consumer for REST and GraphQL APIs.

By default, JavaScript can request resources with `XMLHttpRequest` or `fetch`, as long as the server and the frontend live in the same origin. An origin in HTTP is the combination of the scheme or protocol, the domain, and the port. This means that the origin `http://localhost:8000` is not equal to `http://localhost:3000`. When JavaScript attempts to fetch a resource from a different origin than its own, a mechanism known as *Cross-Origin Resource Sharing* (CORS) kicks in the browser. In any REST or GraphQL project, CORS is necessary to control what origins can connect to the API. To enable CORS in Django, we can install `django-cors-headers` in our project with the following command:

```
pip install django-cors-headers
```

To enable the package, include `corsheaders` in `decoupled_dj/settings/base.py`, as shown in Listing 7-10.

Listing 7-10. decoupled_dj/settings/base.py - Enabling django-cors-headers in Django

```
INSTALLED_APPS = [
    ...
    'corsheaders',
    ...
]
```

Next up, enable the CORS middleware as much higher in the list of middleware, as shown in Listing 7-11.

Listing 7-11. decoupled_dj/settings/base.py - Enabling CORS Middleware

```
MIDDLEWARE = [
    ...
    'corsheaders.middleware.CorsMiddleware',
    'django.middleware.common.CommonMiddleware',
    ...
]
```

With this change in place, we can configure django-cors-headers. In development, we may want to allow all origins to bypass CORS altogether. To decoupled_dj/settings/development.py, add the configuration shown in Listing 7-12.

Listing 7-12. Decoupled_dj/settings/development.py - Relaxing CORS in Development

```
CORS_ALLOW_ALL_ORIGINS = True
```

In production, we have to be more restrictive. django-cors-headers allows us to define a list of allowed origins, which can be configured in decoupled_dj/settings/production.py, as shown in Listing 7-13.

Listing 7-13. decoupled_dj/settings/production.py - Hardening CORS in Production

```
CORS_ALLOWED_ORIGINS = [
    "https://example.com",
    "http://another1.io",
    "http://another2.io",
]
```

Since we are using variables per environment, we can make this configuration directive a list, as shown in Listing 7-14.

Listing 7-14. decoupled_dj/settings/production.py - Hardening CORS in Production

```
CORS_ALLOWED_ORIGINS = env.list(
    "CORS_ALLOWED_ORIGINS",
    default=[]
)
```

This way we can define allowed origins as a comma-separated list in .env for production. CORS is a basic form of protection for users, since without this mechanism in place, any website would be able to fetch and inject malicious code in the page, and a protection for REST APIs, which can explicitly allow a list of predefined origins instead of being open to the world. Of course, CORS does not absolutely replace authentication, which is covered briefly in the next section.

Authentication and Authorization in the DRF

Authentication in the DRF integrates seamlessly with what Django already provides out of the box. By default, the DRF authenticates the user with two classes, SessionAuthentication and BasicAuthentication, aptly named after the two most common authentication methods for websites. Basic authentication is a highly insecure authentication method, even under HTTPS, and it makes sense to disable it altogether to leave enabled at least only session-based authentication. To configure this aspect of the DRF, open decoupled_dj/settings/base.py, add the REST_FRAMEWORK dictionary, and configure the desired authentication classes, as shown in Listing 7-15.

Listing 7-15. decoupled_dj/settings/base.py - Tweaking Authentication for the Django REST Framework

```
REST_FRAMEWORK = {
    "DEFAULT_AUTHENTICATION_CLASSES": [
        "rest_framework.authentication.SessionAuthentication",
    ],
}
```

In web applications, authentication refers to the "who you are?" part of the identification flow. Authorization instead looks at the "what can you do with your credentials" part. In fact, authentication alone is not enough to protect resources in a

101

website or in a REST API. As of now, the REST API for our billing app is open to any user. Specifically, we need to secure two DRF views in `billing/api/views.py`, summarized in Listing 7-16.

Listing 7-16. billing/api/views.py – The DRF View for the Billing App

```
from .serializers import InvoiceSerializer
from .serializers import UserSerializer, User
from rest_framework.generics import CreateAPIView, ListAPIView

class ClientList(ListAPIView):
    serializer_class = UserSerializer
    queryset = User.objects.all()

class InvoiceCreate(CreateAPIView):
    serializer_class = InvoiceSerializer
```

These two views handle the logic for the following endpoints:

- `/billing/api/clients/`

- `/billing/api/invoices/`

Right now, both are accessible by anyone. By default, the DRF does not enforce any form of permission on views. The default permission class is `AllowAny`. To fix the security of all DRF views in the project, we can apply the `IsAdminUser` permission globally. To do so, in `decoupled_dj/settings/base.py`, we augment the `REST_FRAMEWORK` dictionary with a permission class, as shown in Listing 7-17.

Listing 7-17. decoupled_dj/setting/base.py - Adding Permissions Globally in the DRF

```
REST_FRAMEWORK = {
    "DEFAULT_AUTHENTICATION_CLASSES": [
        "rest_framework.authentication.SessionAuthentication",
    ],
    "DEFAULT_PERMISSION_CLASSES": [
        "rest_framework.permissions.IsAdminUser"
    ],
}
```

Permission classes can be set not only globally, but also on a single view, depending on the specific use case.

Note We could also enforce these checks only in `decoupled_dj/settings/production.py`. This means we won't be bothered by authentication in development. However, I prefer to apply authentication and authorization globally to ensure a more realistic scenario, particularly in testing.

Disable the Browsable API

The DRF eases most of the mundane work of building REST APIs. When we create an endpoint, the DRF gives us a free web interface for interacting with the API. For example, for creation views, we can access an HTML form to create new objects through the interface. In this regard, the browsable API is a huge boon for developers because it offers a convenient UI for interacting with the API. However, the interface can potentially leak data and expose too many details if we forget to protect the API. By default, the DRF uses `BrowsableAPIRenderer` to render the browsable API. We can change this behavior by exposing only `JSONRenderer`. This configuration can be placed in `decoupled_dj/settings/production.py`, as shown in Listing 7-18.

Listing 7-18. decoupled_dj/setting/production.py - Disabling the Browsable API in Production

```
...
REST_FRAMEWORK = {**REST_FRAMEWORK,
    "DEFAULT_RENDERER_CLASSES": ["rest_framework.renderers.JSONRenderer"]
}
...
```

This disables the browsable API only in production.

Deploying a Decoupled Django Project

The modern cloud landscape offers endless possibilities to deploy Django.

It would be impossible to cover every single deployment style, not counting Docker, Kubernetes, and serverless setups. Instead, in this section, we employ one of the most traditional setups for Django in production. With the help of Ansible, a popular automation tool, we deploy Django, NGINX, and Gunicorn. Included in the source code for this chapter there is an Ansible playbook, which is helpful to replicate the setup on your own servers. From the preparation of the target machine to the configuration of NGINX, the following sections cover the deployment theory for the project we have built so far.

Note   The source code for the Ansible playbook is at `https://github.com/valentinogagliardi/decoupled-dj/blob/chapter_07_security_deployment/deployment/site.yml`. Instructions on how to launch the playbook can be found in the README.

Preparing the Target Machine

To deploy Django, we need all the required packages in place: NGINX, Git, a newer version of Python, and Certbot for requesting SSL certificates.

The Ansible playbook covers the installation of these packages. In this chapter, we skip the installation of Postgres to keep things simple. The reader is encouraged to check the PostgreSQL download page to see the installation instructions. On the target system, there should also be an unprivileged user for the Django project. Once you're done with these prerequisites, you can move to configure NGINX, the reverse proxy.

Note   The Ansible playbook expects Ubuntu as the operating system used for the deployment; a version not older than Ubuntu 20.04 LTS is enough.

Configuring NGINX

In a typical production arrangement, NGINX works at the edge of the system.

It receives requests from the users, deals with SSL, and forwards these requests to a WSGI or ASGI server. Django lives behind this curtain. To configure NGINX, in this example, we use the domain name decoupled-django.com and the subdomain static. decoupled-django.com. The NGINX configuration for a typical Django project is composed of three sections at least:

- One or more upstream declarations

- A server declaration for the main Django entry point

- A server declaration for serving static files

The deployment/templates/decoupled-django.com.j2 file includes the whole configuration; here we outline just some details of the setup. The upstream directive instructs NGINX about the location of the WSGI/ASGI server. Listing 7-19 shows the relevant configuration.

Listing 7-19. deployment/templates/decoupled-django.com.j2 - Upstream Configuration for NGINX

```
upstream gunicorn {
    server 127.0.0.1:8000;
}
```

In the first server block, we tell NGINX to forward all the requests for the main domain to the upstream, as shown in Listing 7-20.

Listing 7-20. deployment/templates/decoupled-django.com.j2 - Server Configuration for NGINX

```
server {
    server_name {{ domain }};

    location / {
        proxy_pass http://gunicorn;
        proxy_set_header Host $host;
        proxy_set_header X-Real-IP $remote_addr;
```

```
        proxy_set_header X-Forwarded-For $proxy_add_x_forwarded_for;
        proxy_set_header X-Forwarded-Proto $scheme;
    }

    ## SSL configuration is managed by Certbot
}
```

Here {{ domain }} is an Ansible variable declared in the playbook. What's important here is the `proxy_pass` directive, which forwards requests to Gunicorn. In addition, in this section we also set headers for the proxy, which are handed down to Django on each request. In particular, we have:

- `X-Real-IP` and `X-Forwarded-For`, which ensure that Django gets the IP address of the real visitor, not the address of the proxy

- `X-Forwarded-Proto`, which tells Django which protocol the client is connecting with (HTTP or HTTPS)

Gunicorn and Django Production Requirements

In Chapter 3, we introduced asynchronous Django, and we used Uvicorn to run Django locally under ASGI. In production, we may want to run Uvicorn with Gunicorn. To do so, we need to configure our dependencies for production. In the `requirements` folder, create a new file named `production.txt`. In this file, we declare all the dependencies for the ASGI part, as shown in Listing 7-21.

Listing 7-21. requirements/production.txt - Production Requirements

```
-r ./base.txt
gunicorn==20.0.4
uvicorn==0.13.1
httptools==0.1.1
uvloop==0.15.2
```

This file should land in the Git repo, as it will be used in the deployment phase. Let's now see how to prepare our Vue.js app for production.

Preparing Vue.js in Production with Django

In Chapter 6, we saw how to serve Vue.js under Django in development. We configured `vue.config.js`, and a file named `.env.staging` inside the root folder of the Vue.js app. This time, we are going to ship things in production. This means we need a production Vue.js bundle which should be served by NGINX, not from Django anymore. In regard to static files, in production Django wants to know where it can find JavaScript and CSS. This is configured in `STATIC_URL`, as in Listing 7-22, extracted from the beginning of this chapter.

Listing 7-22. decoupled_dj/settings/.env.production.example - Static Configuration for Production

```
...
STATIC_URL=https://static.decoupled-django.com/
STATIC_ROOT=static/
...
```

Notice that we use `https://static.decoupled-django.com`, and this subdomain must be configured in NGINX. Listing 7-23 shows the subdomain configuration.

Listing 7-23. deployment/templates/decoupled-django.com.j2 - Ansible Template for NGINX

```
...
server {
    server_name static.{{ domain }};

    location / {
        alias /home/{{ user }}/code/static/;
    }
}
...
```

Here, `{{ user }}` is another variable defined in the Ansible playbook. After setting up Django and NGINX, to configure Vue.js so that it "knows" that it will be served from the above subdomain, we need to create another environment file in `billing/vue_spa`, named `.env.production` with the content shown in Listing 7-24.

Listing 7-24. billing/vue_spa/.env.production - Production Configuration for Vue.js

```
VUE_APP_STATIC_URL=https://static.decoupled-django.com/billing/
```

This tells Vue.js that its bundle will be served from a specific subdomain/path. With the file in place, if we move to the `billing/vue_spa` folder, we can run the following command:

```
npm run build -- --mode production
```

This will build the optimized Vue.js bundle in `static/billing`. We now need to push these files to the Git repo. After doing so, in the next section we finally see how to deploy the project starting right from this repo.

Note   In real-world projects, production JavaScript bundles are not directly pushed to source control. Instead, a continuous integration/deployment system takes care of building production assets, or Docker images, after all the test suites pass.

The Deployment

After building Vue for production locally and committing the files to the repo, we need to deploy the actual code to the target machine.

To do so, we log in as the unprivileged user created in the previous steps (the Ansible playbook defines a user called `decoupled-django`) or with SSH. Once done, we clone the repo to a folder, which can be called `code` for convenience:

```
git clone --branch chapter_07_security_deployment https://github.com/
valentinogagliardi/decoupled-dj.git code
```

This command clones the repo for the project from the specified branch `chapter_07_security_deployment`. When the code is in place, we move to the newly created folder, and we activate a Python virtual environment:

```
cd code
python3.8 -m venv venv
source venv/bin/activate
```

Next up, we install production dependencies with the following command:

```
pip install -r requirements/production.txt
```

Before running Django, we need to configure the environment file for production. This file must be placed in decoupled_dj/settings/.env. Extra care must be taken when managing this file, as it contains sensitive credentials and the Django secret key. In particular, .env files should never land in source control. Listing 7-25 recaps the configuration directive for the production environment.

Listing 7-25. decoupled_dj/settings/.env.production.example - Environment Variables for Production

```
ALLOWED_HOSTS=decoupled-django.com,static.decoupled-django.com
DEBUG=no
SECRET_KEY=!changethis!
DATABASE_URL=psql://decoupleddjango:localpassword@127.0.0.1/decoupleddjango
STATIC_URL=https://static.decoupled-django.com/
STATIC_ROOT=static/
```

An example of this file is available in the source repo in decoupled_dj/settings/.env.production.example. With this file in place, we can switch Django to production with the following command:

```
export DJANGO_SETTINGS_MODULE=decoupled_dj.settings.production
```

Finally, we can collect static assets with collectstatic and apply migrations:

```
python manage.py collectstatic --noinput
python manage.py migrate
```

The first command will copy static files to /home/decoupled-django/code/static, which are picked up by NGINX. In the Ansible playbook there is a series of tasks to automate all the steps presented here. Before running the project, we can create a superuser to access protected routes:

```
python manage.py createsuperuser
```

To test things out, still in /home/decoupled-django/code, we can run Gunicorn with the following command:

```
gunicorn decoupled_dj.asgi:application -w 2 -k uvicorn.workers.
UvicornWorker -b 127.0.0.1:8000 --log-file -
```

The Ansible playbook also includes a Systemd service for setting up Gunicorn at boot. If everything goes well, we can access https://decoupled-django.com/77randomAdmin@33/, log in to the website with the superuser credentials, and visit https://decoupled-django.com/billing/, where our Vue.js app lives. Figure 7-1 shows the result of our work.

Figure 7-1. *Django and the Vue.js app deployed in production*

Again, the Ansible playbook covers the deployment from the Git repo as well. For most projects, Ansible is a good starting point to set up and deploy your Django projects. Other alternatives these days are Docker and Kubernetes, which more and more teams have fully internalized into their deployment toolchains.

> **Note**   It is a good moment to commit the changes you made so far, and to push the work to your Git repo. You can find the source code for this chapter at `https://github.com/valentinogagliardi/decoupled-dj/tree/chapter_07_security_deployment`.

Summary

We covered a lot in this chapter. We went over security and deployment. In the process, you learned that:

- Django is quite secure by default, but extra measures must be taken when exposing a REST API

- Django doesn't work alone; a reverse proxy like NGINX is a must for production setups

- There are many ways to deploy Django; a configuration tool like Ansible can work well in most cases

In the next chapter, we cover how Next.js, the React Framework, can be used as a frontend for Django.

Additional Resource

- OWASP REST Security Cheat Sheet

CHAPTER 8

Django REST Meets Next.js

This chapter covers:

- Django as a content repo

- React and its ecosystem

- Vue.js and its ecosystem in brief

After having touched on security and deployment, in this chapter, we go back to our local workstation to build a blog with Next.js, the React production framework, and TypeScript.

Django as a Headless CMS

Decoupled architectures based on REST and GraphQL have facilitated the rise in recent years of a new trend: that of headless CMS.

With a backend that exclusively handles the data and serialization of the input/output, we can create consumer frontends that are totally decoupled from the backend. These frontends are not limited only to act as single-page applications, but can also retrieve data from the backend to build static websites. In this chapter, we introduce Next.js, a React framework for server-side rendering and static site generation.

Building the Blog App

There are countless books and tutorials on Django that use a blog application as the most straightforward way to introduce beginners to this fantastic framework.

It might not be the most exciting application ever, but in our case it turns out to be a perfect candidate for using Django as a content repository with JavaScript frameworks. Let's get started.

© Valentino Gagliardi 2021
V. Gagliardi, *Decoupled Django*, https://doi.org/10.1007/978-1-4842-7144-5_8

> **Note**   This chapter assumes you are in the repo root `decoupled-dj`, with
> the Python virtual environment active and the environment variable `DJANGO_`
> `SETTINGS_MODULE` set to `decoupled_dj.settings.development`.

Building the Model

For our blog app, we need a `Blog` model. This model should be connected to a `User`.
Each `User` should also be able to access its blog posts. To start off, we create the model in
`blog/models.py`, as shown in Listing 8-1.

Listing 8-1. blog/models.py - Model for the Blog App

```python
from django.db import models
from django.conf import settings

class Blog(models.Model):
    class Status(models.TextChoices):
        PUBLISHED = "PUBLISHED"
        UNPUBLISHED = "UNPUBLISHED"

    user = models.ForeignKey(
        to=settings.AUTH_USER_MODEL,
        on_delete=models.PROTECT,
        related_name="blog_posts"
    )
    title = models.CharField(max_length=160)
    body = models.TextField()
    status = models.CharField(
        max_length=15,
        choices=Status.choices,
        default=Status.UNPUBLISHED
    )
    created_at = models.DateTimeField(auto_now_add=True)
```

In this model, we define some of the most common fields for a blog entry:

- title: The title for the blog entry

- body: The text of the blog entry

- created_at: The creation date

- status: Whether the entry is published or unpublished

On the user field we have a foreign key to User, with related_name aptly configured so that the user can access its posts via the .blog_posts attribute in the ORM. We could add much more fields, like a slug, but for the scope of this chapter, these are enough.

Enabling the App

With the model in place, we enable the app in decoupled_dj/settings/base.py, as in Listing 8-2.

Listing 8-2. decoupled_dj/settings/base.py - Enabling the Blog App

```
INSTALLED_APPS = [
    ...
    "blog.apps.BlogConfig",
]
```

Finally, we apply the migrations:

```
python manage.py makemigrations
python manage.py migrate
```

While we are there, let's create a couple of blog entries in the database. First we open a Django shell:

```
python manage.py shell_plus
```

Then we create the entries (>>> is the shell prompt):

```
>>> juliana = User.objects.create_user(username="jul81", name="Juliana",
email="juliana@acme.io")
>>> Blog.objects.create(title="Exploring Next.js", body="Dummy body",
user=juliana)
>>> Blog.objects.create(title="Decoupled Django", body="Dummy body", user=juliana)
```

We will need these entries later, so this step can't be skipped. With the app in place, we are now ready to build the REST logic before moving on.

Building the REST Backend

Our goal is to expose the Blog model to the outside. By doing so, any JavaScript client can retrieve blog entries. As we did in Chapter 5 with the billing app, we need to wire up the foundations of the DRF: serializers and views. In the next section, we build a serializer for Blog and two views for exposing blog entries.

Building the Serializer

To structure our REST API, we create a new Python package named api in blog. In this package we place all the logic for our REST API. To start, let's create a new file at blog/api/serializers.py with the serializer in Listing 8-3.

Listing 8-3. blog/api/serializers.py - DRF Serializer for the Blog Model

```
from blog.models import Blog
from rest_framework import serializers

class BlogSerializer(serializers.ModelSerializer):
    class Meta:
        model = Blog
        fields = ["title",
                  "body",
                  "created_at",
                  "status",
                  "id"]
```

There is nothing arcane in this serializer: it exposes the fields of the model, minus user. Save and close the file. With the serializer in place, we can build views and the URL configuration.

Building the Views and the URL

For this project we need two views:

- A ListAPIView to expose the whole list of posts

- A RetrieveAPIView to expose single entries

We create views in a new file at blog/api/views.py, as shown in Listing 8-4.

Listing 8-4. blog/api/views.py - REST Views for Our Blog

```python
from .serializers import BlogSerializer
from blog.models import Blog
from rest_framework.generics import ListAPIView, RetrieveAPIView

class BlogList(ListAPIView):
    serializer_class = BlogSerializer
    queryset = Blog.objects.all()

class BlogDetail(RetrieveAPIView):
    serializer_class = BlogSerializer
    queryset = Blog.objects.all()
```

Next up, we create a URL configuration in a new file at blog/urls.py. As usual, we give this configuration an app_name, which is useful to namespace the app in the root URL configuration, as shown in Listing 8-5.

Listing 8-5. blog/urls.py - URL Configuration for the Blog App

```python
from django.urls import path
from .api.views import BlogList, BlogDetail

app_name = "blog"

urlpatterns = [
    path("api/posts/",
        BlogList.as_view(),
        name="list"),
```

```
path("api/posts/<int:pk>",
    BlogDetail.as_view(),
    name="detail"),
]
```

Finally, we include the URL configuration for our blog in decoupled_dj/urls.py, as shown in Listing 8-6.

Listing 8-6. blog/urls.py - Project URL Configuration

```
from django.urls import path, include

urlpatterns = [
    ...
    path("blog/", include("blog.urls", namespace="blog")),
]
```

After running the Django development server, we should be able to access the endpoint at http://localhost:8000/blog/api/posts/. This will be the data source for Next.js.

Note   To avoid being bothered by authentication in this chapter, you can temporarily comment DEFAULT_PERMISSION_CLASSES in decoupled_dj/ setting/base.py.

Introduction to the React Ecosystem

React is a JavaScript library for building user interfaces that took web development by storm.

The React approach to building user interfaces by the means of components, isolated units of markup, and JavaScript code is not new to the scene. However, thanks to its flexibility, React gained huge popularity, surpassing Angular and Vue.js as the library of choice for building single-page apps. In the next sections, we recap React fundamentals and introduce Next.js, the React framework for production.

A Reintroduction to React

Most of the time, user interfaces are not a single whole: they are made of independent units, each one in control of a specific aspect of the whole interface.

If we think of a `<select>` HTML element for example, we may notice that in a typical application it rarely appears just once. Instead, it can be used multiple times in the same interface. In the beginning, web developers (myself included) reused part of the application by copy-pasting the same markup over and over. However, this approach often led to an unsustainable mess. In the past the question was: "How do I reuse this markup alongside with its JavaScript logic"? React filled this huge gap, which still affects the web platform to some extent: the lack of native components, that is, reusable pieces of markup and logic.

Note   It is worth noting that Web Components (native components for building interfaces) are a reality, but the specification still has a lot of rough edges.

React favors a component-based approach to building user interfaces. In the beginning, React components were built as ES2015 classes due to their ability to retain internal state. With the advent of hooks, a React component can be built as a simple JavaScript function, as in Listing 8-7.

Listing 8-7. React Component Example

```
import React, { useState } from "react";

export default function Button(props) {
 const [text, setText] = useState("");
 return (
   <button onClick={() => setText("CLICKED")}>
     {text || props.initialText}
   </button>
 );
}
```

In this example we define a `Button` component as a JavaScript function. In the component we use the `useState` hook to hold the internal state. When we click on the button, the `onClick` handler (which React maps to the `click` DOM event) triggers `setText()`, which changes the internal state of the component. Additionally, the component takes `props` from the outside, that is, a read-only object that takes an arbitrary number of properties that the component can use to render data to the user. Once we create a component, we can reuse it infinitely, as shown in Listing 8-8.

Listing 8-8. React Component Usage Example

```
import Button from "./Button";

export default function App() {
 return (

     <Button initialText="CLICK ME" />
     <Button initialText="CLICK ME" />

 );
}
```

Here we have an `App` root component that nests our `Button` two times. From the outside we pass an `initialText` property. React components are not always that simple, but this example summarizes the grand theory of React and serves to pave the road for the next sections.

Introduction to Next.js

Building single-page applications might look easy. We became accustomed to using tools like create-react-app and Vue CLI to create new SPA projects.

These tools give the illusion that the work is done, which is true to some extent. The reality is that things are not so straightforward in production. Depending on the project, we need routing, efficient data fetching, search engine optimization, internationalization, and performance and image optimization. Next.js is a framework for React, born to ease the burden of setting up things manually over and over again, and to provide developers with an opinionated production-ready environment.

In Chapter 2, we talked briefly about universal JavaScript applications, touching on the ability to share and reuse code between the backend and frontend. Next.js falls exactly in this category of tools, as it enables developers to write server-side rendered JavaScript applications. Next.js has two principal modes of operation:

- Server-side rendering
- Static site generation

In the next sections, we investigate both while building our blog frontend with React and TypeScript. It's important to remark that these kinds of frameworks cannot directly integrate with Django because they have their own server, operated by Node.js. A typical Next.js setup operates independently of any other backend; it handles routing, authentication, internationalization, and everything in between. In this arrangement, a framework like Django provides just the data for Next.js over a REST or GraphQL API.

Building the Next.js Frontend

To start, we initialize a Next.js project. From the root project folder decoupled_dj/, launch the following command:

```
npx create-next-app --use-npm next-blog
```

This will create the project in decoupled_dj/next-blog. Once the project is in place, move into the folder:

```
cd next-blog
```

From inside the Next.js project folder, install TypeScript and a couple of other type definitions, one for Node,js and another for React:

```
npm i typescript @types/react @types/node --save-dev
```

When the installation finishes, create a configuration file for TypeScript with the following command:

```
touch tsconfig.json
```

In this file, depending on the level of strictness we want TypeScript to enforce, we can leave the strict option set to false. However, for most projects we may want to set it to true. With the file in place, launch the Next.js development server:

```
npm run dev
```

This will start Next.js on `http://localhost:3000`. If everything goes well, you should see the following output from the console:

```
ready - started server on 0.0.0.0:3000, url: http://localhost:3000
We detected TypeScript in your project and created a tsconfig.json file for
you.
```

From there, we are ready to write our first component.

Pages and Routing

The basic theory of Next.js revolves around the concept of pages.

If we look in the newly created project, we should see a folder named `pages`. In this folder, we can define subfolders. For example, by creating a new folder at `pages/posts`, when running the Next.js project, we can access `http://localhost:3000/posts/`. Nothing particularly exciting. The interesting part comes with React components. Any `.js`, `.jsx`, `.ts`, or `.tsx` file placed in `pages` becomes a page for Next.js. To understand how Next.js works, we create a page step by step by starting with fixed data first, to introduce data fetching later.

Note   For the Next.js part, from now on we work in `decoupled_dj/next-blog`. Each proposed file must be created in the appropriate subfolder, starting from this path.

We are going to create a simple page in Next.js. For the following example, create a new file in `pages/posts/index.tsx`, with the following React component shown in Listing 8-9.

Listing 8-9.   pages/posts/index.tsx - A First Next.js Page

```
const BlogPost = () => {
 return (
   <div>
     <h1>Post title</h1>
     <div>
       <p>Post body</p>
     </div>
```

```
      </div>
  );
};
```

```
export default BlogPost;
```

This is a React component, and it's also already a page for Next.js. Let's run the development server:

```
npm run dev
```

Now, we can head over to `http://localhost:3000/posts`, and we should be able to see a simple page with the content we placed in the React component. Interesting indeed, but a bit useless for a dynamic website. What if we want to show different blog posts, maybe by fetching them by `id`?

In Next.js, we can use *dynamic routing* to build pages on demand. For example, a user should be able to access `http://localhost:3000/posts/2` and see the desired content there. For this to work, we need to change the filename of our component from `index.ts` to the following:

```
[id].tsx
```

By doing so, Next.js will respond to any request for `http://localhost:3000/posts/$id` where $id here is a placeholder for whichever numeric ID we can imagine. With this information, the component can fetch data from the REST API, based on the id, which for Next.js becomes a URL parameter. With this knowledge, let's enrich the component with type declarations before moving to data fetching. Wipe everything out from the component we created a minute ago and place the following code in `pages/posts/[id].tsx`, as shown in Listing 8-10.

Listing 8-10. pages/posts/[id]tsx - Blog Component for the Corresponding Next.js Page

```
enum BlogPostStatus {
 Published = "PUBLISHED",
 Unpublished = "UNPUBLISHED",
}
```

```
type BlogPost = {
 title: string;
```

```
 body: string;
 created_at: string;
 status: BlogPostStatus;
 id: number;
};

const BlogPost = ({ title, body, created_at }: BlogPost) => {
 return (
   <div>
     <header>
       <h1>{title} </h1>
       <span>Published on: {created_at}</span>
     </header>
     <div>
       <p>{body}</p>
     </div>
   </div>
 );
};

export default BlogPost;
```

This component is statically typed with TypeScript. There are three specific TypeScript notations in this file. Here's an explanation:

- BlogPostStatus: TypeScript enum that defines a set of possible states for the blog post. It maps the nested Status class defined in the Django model.

- BlogPost: TypeScript type that defines the properties for our React component. It maps the model's fields (minus user).

- BlogPost: Used in the component parameter to strongly type our props.

With this component in place, we are now ready to define the data fetching logic to populate each blog post with its corresponding data.

> **Note**   In TypeScript, enums produce a lot of JavaScript code during compilation. A solution to this are const enums, but they are not supported by Babel, which Next. js uses for compiling TypeScript to JavaScript.

Data Fetching

Next.js can operate in two modes, as introduced earlier:

- Server-side rendering

- Static site generation

With server-side rendering, pages are built on each request, much like a traditional server-side rendered website. Think of Django templates or Rails. In this mode, we can fetch data on each request, as the user hits the corresponding path. In Next.js this is done with getServerSideProps. This should be an asynchronous method, exported from the same file where the React component lives. There are two things we need to take care of in getServerSideProps:

- Fetch the desired data

- Return at least a props object

Once these are done, Next.js will take care of passing props to our React component. Listing 8-11 shows an example skeleton of the function, complete with types.

Listing 8-11. getServerSideProps Skeleton

```
export const getServerSideProps: GetServerSideProps = async (context) => {
 // fetch data
 return { props: {} };
};
```

The context object parameter carries information about the request, the response, and a params object on which we can access the request parameters. We will destructure params from context for convenience. Let's add this function to pages/posts/[id].tsx, as shown in Listing 8-12, with the corresponding data fetching logic.

Listing 8-12. pages/posts/[id].tsx - Data Fetching Logic for the Page

```
import { GetServerSideProps } from "next";

const BASE_URL = "http://localhost:8000/blog/api";

export const getServerSideProps: GetServerSideProps = async ({ params }) =>
{
 const id = params?.id;

 const res = await fetch(`${BASE_URL}/posts/${id}`);

 if (!res.ok) {
   return {
     notFound: true,
   };
 }

 const json = await res.json();
 const { title, body, created_at, status } = json;

 return { props: { title, body, created_at, status } };
};
```

This code bears a bit of explanation:

- We import the GetServerSideProps type, which is used to give typing to the actual function

- In getServerSideProps:

    - We get the id from params

    - We fetch data from the Django REST API

    - We return notFound if the response from the API is negative

    - We return a props object for our component if the backend returns the blog post

---

Note   getServerSideProps has a lot more return properties, which are convenient for specific use cases. Take a look at the official documentation to learn more.

With this code in place, we can test things out. First off, Django must be running. In a terminal, go to decoupled_dj and launch Django:

```
python manage.py runserver
```

In the other terminal where you launched Next.js, run the development server if it isn't already running (from the decoupled_dj/next_blog folder):

```
npm run dev
```

Now, access http://localhost:3000/posts/1 or http://localhost:3000/posts/2. You should see a blog post, as shown in Figure 8-1.

Decoupled Django

Published on: 2021-02-17T16:33:32.710992Z

Dummy body

Figure 8-1. Next.js is responding to the detail route for a single blog post

As you can see, this approach works flawlessly. In this mode, Next.js retrieves data before sending the page to the user. But for a blog, this is not the best approach: there is no better website than a static website for making search engines happy. The next section explains how to implement data fetching and static site generation with Next.js.

Static Site Generation

It's a bit inefficient to call the REST API every time we want to display a blog post to our users.

Blogs are better served as static pages. Other than data fetching on each request, Next.js supports also data fetching at build time. In this mode we can generate pages and their corresponding data as static HTML, which Next.js will serve to our users. To make this work, we need a combination of two other methods from Next.js: getStaticPaths and getStaticProps. What's the difference between getServerSideProps from the previous section and these methods?

getServerSideProps is used to asynchronously fetch data on each request in server-side rendering. That is, when the user reaches a given page, it has to wait a bit because the Next.js server has to fetch the data from the given sources (a REST API or a GraphQL service). This approach is convenient for data that is dynamic and changes a lot.

getStaticProps, instead, is used to asynchronously fetch data at build time. That is, when we run npm run build or yarn build, Next.js creates a production bundle with all the JavaScript it needs, plus any page marked as static. Listing 8-13 shows an example skeleton of the function.

Listing 8-13. getStaticProps Example

```
import { GetStaticProps } from "next";

const BASE_URL = "http://localhost:8000/blog/api";

export const getStaticProps: GetStaticProps = async (_) => {
 const res = await fetch(`${BASE_URL}/posts/1`);

 const json = await res.json();
 const { title, body, created_at, status } = json;

 return { props: { title, body, created_at, status } };
};
```

Notice how we call http://localhost:8000/blog/api/1 specifically, which is rather limiting. After the build phase, Next.js generates the corresponding static pages. By running npm run start or yarn start, Next.js can serve our website. When a page exports getStaticProps, the related component receives props returned from this method. However, to make our example work, the page must have a fixed path, like

1.tsx. It would be impractical to know beforehand the ID of every blog post in our backend. This is where getStaticPaths comes into play. With this method, used in combination with getStaticProps, we can generate a list of paths that getStaticProps can use to fetch data. To take advantage of static site generation, let's change pages/posts/[id].tsx so that it uses getStaticPaths and getStaticProps instead of getServerSideProps, as shown in Listing 8-14.

Listing 8-14. pages/posts/[id].tsx - Data Fetching at Build Time with getStaticPaths and getStaticProps

```
import { GetStaticPaths, GetStaticProps } from "next";

const BASE_URL = "http://localhost:8000/blog/api";

export const getStaticPaths: GetStaticPaths = async (_) => {
  const res = await fetch(`${BASE_URL}/posts/`);
  const json: BlogPost[] = await res.json();
  const paths = json.map((post) => {
    return { params: { id: String(post.id) } };
  });

  return {
    paths,
    fallback: false,
  };
};

export const getStaticProps: GetStaticProps = async ({ params }) => {
  const id = params?.id;

  const res = await fetch(`${BASE_URL}/posts/${id}`);

  if (!res.ok) {
    return {
      notFound: true,
    };
  }
```

```
const json: BlogPost = await res.json();
const { title, body, created_at, status } = json;

return { props: { title, body, created_at, status } };
};
```

Here, the logic for getStaticProps is the same used for getServerSideProps from the previous section. However, we also have getStaticPaths. In this function, we:

- Call the REST API to get a list of all posts from http://127.0.0.1:8000/blog/api/posts/

- Generate and return an array of paths

This array of paths is important and must have the following shape:

```
paths: [
  { params: { id: 1 } },
  { params: { id: 2 } },
  { params: { id: 3 } },
]
```

In our code it is generated by the following snippet:

```
...
const paths = json.map((post) => {
  return { params: { id: String(post.id) } };
});
...
```

In the return object for getStaticPaths, there is also a fallback option. It's used to display a 404 page for any path not included in paths. At this point we can build the blog with the following command:

```
npm run build
```

Note that Django must still be running in another terminal. Once the build is ready, we should see static pages in .next/server/pages/posts. To serve the blog (at least locally for now), we run the following command:

```
npm run start
```

Now, access `http://localhost:3000/posts/1` or `http://localhost:3000/posts/2` and you should see a blog post, as shown in Figure 8-1. Apparently, nothing changes for the user between this version and the previous version with `getServerSideProps`. But if we stop the Django API, we can still access our blog, since now it's just a bunch of static pages, and more important, the performance gains of static HTML can't be beaten.

Note   `getStaticProps` and `getServerSideProps` are not mutually exclusive. Pages in a Next.js project can use both depending on the use case. For example, part of a site can be served as static HTML, while another section can operate as a single-page application.

We covered a lot. The concept exposed here might seem a bit too much seen in the context of a simple blog. After all, Django alone would be enough to handle this type of website. But more and more teams are adopting these kinds of setups, where frontend developers can use the tool they love most to shape the UI, ranging from single-page apps to static websites.

Deploying Next.js

Next.js is a full-fledged React framework. It needs its own Node.js server, which is already integrated, and this also means it can't run inside Django. Usually, the deployment is structured to have a Django backend and the Next.js system on their own separate machines/containers.

Using React with Django

In 2019, I published a post on my blog entitled, "Django REST with React."

The tutorial illustrates how to configure a webpack environment to build React in the right Django static folder, much like we did in Chapter 5 with Vue.js. The approach outlined in that blog post is not inherently bad, but it can fall short for larger teams, and due to potential breaking changes in webpack, it can become hard to keep up with changes. A solution to this is the popular create-react-app, which abstracts away all the mundane details related to webpack and Babel. However, to make Django work with create-react-app, Django must be instructed to look for React static files. This involves tweaking the `DIRS` key in `TEMPLATES` and `STATICFILES_DIRS`.

The Vue.js Ecosystem

To a casual observer, the modern web development land might seem totally dominated by React.

That couldn't be further from the truth. Vue.js and Angular occupy a good market share. Vue.js has a framework called Nuxt.js, equivalent in functionality to Next.js. There isn't enough space to cover everything in this book, but given that Next.js and Nuxt.js have almost total feature parity, developers accustomed to working with Vue.js can apply the same concepts seen in this chapter to their framework of choice. In fact, you're encouraged to give Nuxt.js a try.

Note It is a good moment to commit the changes you made so far and to push the work to your Git repo. You can find the source code for this chapter at `https://github.com/valentinogagliardi/decoupled-dj/tree/chapter_08_django_rest_meets_next`.

Summary

This chapter paired a Next.js project to the blog app REST API. In the process, you learned about:

- TypeScript for React
- Next.js operation modes
- Next.js data fetching

In the next chapter, we get even more serious with unit and functional testing for the whole spectrum, from backend to frontend.

Additional Resource

- Next.js docs

CHAPTER 9

Testing in a Decoupled World

This chapter covers:

- Functional testing for JavaScript-heavy interfaces

- Unit testing for the Django REST Framework

In this chapter, we add tests to our application. In the first part, we cover functional testing for user interfaces with Cypress. In the second part, we move to unit testing in Django.

Note This chapter assumes you are in the repo root `decoupled-dj`, with the Python virtual environment active.

Introduction to Functional Testing

More often than not, testing in software development is an afterthought, something overlooked as a waste of time that slows down development.

This is especially true of functional testing for user interfaces, where the amount of JavaScript interactions to test increases day by day. This feeling probably comes from the memory of tools like Selenium for Python, which unfortunately are notably slow and hard to use for testing JavaScript interfaces. However, the situation has changed substantially in recent years, with a new breed of JavaScript tooling that eases the burden of testing single-page applications. These tools make it easy to write tests for the interface from the user point of view. Functional tests are also a great way to catch

© Valentino Gagliardi 2021
V. Gagliardi, *Decoupled Django*, https://doi.org/10.1007/978-1-4842-7144-5_9

regressions in the UI, that is, bugs introduced by accidents during development in an unrelated feature which used to work well before changes. In the next sections, we cover Cypress, a test runner for JavaScript.

Getting Started with Cypress

Cypress is a JavaScript package available on NPM that can be pulled in our projects. In a project with a single JavaScript frontend that needs to be tested, you can install Cypress in the root project folder of the React/Vue.js app.

In our case, since we might have more than one JavaScript application to test, we can install Cypress in the root project folder `decoupled-dj`. To start, initialize a `package.json` with the following command:

```
npm init -y
```

Next up, install Cypress:

```
npm i cypress --save-dev
```

Once you're done, you can start Cypress the first time with the following command:

```
./node_modules/.bin/cypress open
```

This command will open a window and create a new folder named `cypress` in the root project folder. A number of subfolders are created as well, as shown in the following directory listing:

```
cypress
├── fixtures
├── integration
├── plugins
└── support
```

For the scope of this chapter we can safely ignore these folders, except `integration`. We will place our tests there. With Cypress in place, we can move to writing our first test in the next sections.

Understanding Functional Testing for the Billing App

Remember the billing app from Chapter 6? It's now time to write functional tests for it.

This app has a form where the user can fill in fields to create a new invoice and then click on Create Invoice to create the new entity on the backend. Figure 9-1 shows the final form from Chapter 6.

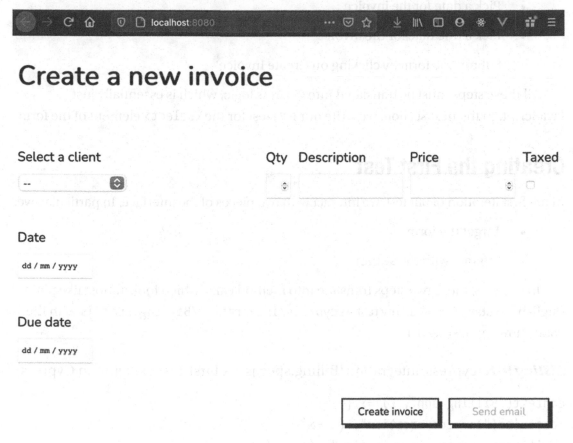

Figure 9-1. *The invoice form from Chapter 6*

Let's not forget that we want to test the interface from the user point of view in a functional test. With a nice fluent syntax, Cypress allows us to interact with elements just like a user would do, step by step. How do we know how and what to test? Writing a functional test should come naturally. We need to imagine how a user would interact with the interface, write selectors for each HTML element we want to test, and then verify that the element behaves correctly or that it changes in response to user interaction. In the case of our form, we can identify the following steps. The user should:

- Select a client for the invoice

- Compile at least one invoice line with quantity, description, and price

- Pick a date for the invoice

- Pick a due date for the invoice

- Submit the form by clicking on Create Invoice

All these steps must be translated into Cypress logic, which is essentially just JavaScript. In the next section, we write our first test for the <select> element of the form.

Creating the First Test

In the first iteration of our test, we interact with two pieces of the interface. In particular, we:

- Target the form

- Interact with the select

In Cypress, these two steps translate into method calls, which look almost like plain English. To start, create a new test in cypress/integration/Billing.spec.js with the code shown in Listing 9-1.

Listing 9-1. cypress/integration/Billing.spec.js - A First Test Skeleton in Cypress

```
context("Billing app", () => {
 describe("Invoice creation", () => {
   it("can create a new invoice", () => {
     cy.visit("http://localhost:8080/"
);
     cy.get("form").within(() => {
       cy.get("select").select("Juliana - juliana@acme.io");
     });
   });
 });
});
```

Let's break down these instructions:

- `context()` encloses the whole test and gives it a cohesive organization

- `describe()` encloses a single aspect of our test, often used in conjunction with `context()`

- `it()` is the actual test block

- `cy.visit()` navigates to the app home page

- `cy` is Cypress itself, which offers a number of methods for selecting and interacting with elements

- `cy.get("form")` selects the first form in the interface

- `within()` tells Cypress to run each subsequent command from inside the previous selected element

- `cy.get("select")` selects the `<select>` element inside the form

- `cy.get("select").select("Juliana - juliana@acme.io")` picks the `<option>` element whose value is `"Juliana - juliana@acme.io"` from the `select`

Note   Since our interface is rather simple, we won't focus too much on advanced selectors and best practices. The reader is encouraged to read the Cypress documentation to learn more about advanced techniques.

What stands out from this code is the expressiveness of each statement. With fluent, descriptive methods, we can target and interact with HTML elements the same way as we would expect from our users. In theory, our test is ready to run, but there's a problem. The `<select>` needs data from the network. This data comes from the Vue component's `mounted()` method, as shown in Listing 9-2.

Listing 9-2. billing/vue_spa/src/components/InvoiceCreate.vue - The Form's Mounted Method

```
...
 mounted() {
   fetch("/billing/api/clients/")
     .then(response => {
       if (!response.ok) throw Error(response.statusText);
       return response.json();
     })
     .then(json => {
       this.users = json;
     });
 }
...
```

In fact, if we launch the Vue.js app, we'll see the following error in the console:

```
Proxy error: Could not proxy request /billing/api/clients/ from
localhost:8080 to http://localhost:8000
```

This comes from Vue.js development server, which we instructed to proxy all network requests to the Django REST API in development. Without running Django in another terminal, we can't really test anything. This is where Cypress network interception comes into play. It turns out that we can intercept the network call and reply to it directly from Cypress. To do so, we need to adjust our test by adding a new command called `cy.intercept()`, before `cy.visit()`, as shown in Listing 9-3.

Listing 9-3. cypress/integration/Billing.spec.js - Adding Network Interception to the Test

```
context("Billing app", () => {
 describe("Invoice creation", () => {
   it("can create a new invoice", () => {
     cy.intercept("GET", "/billing/api/clients", {
       statusCode: 200,
       body: [
```

```
        {
          id: 1,
          name: "Juliana",
          email: "juliana@acme.io",
        },
      ],
    });

    cy.visit("http://localhost:8080/");
    cy.get("form").within(() => {
      cy.get("select").select(
        "Juliana - juliana@acme.io"
      );
    });
  });
});
});
```

From this snippet, we can see that `cy.intercept()` takes:

- The HTTP method to intercept

- The path to intercept

- An object used as a response stub

In this test we intercept the network request coming from the Vue component, we stop it before it reaches the backend, and we reply with a static response body. By doing so, we can avoid touching the backend altogether. Now, to test things out, we can run the test suite. From the `decoupled-dj` folder where we installed Cypress, we run the testing runner with the following command:

```
./node_modules/.bin/cypress open
```

Note   For convenience, it's best to create an e2e script in `package.json` to alias `cypress open`.

This will open a new window from where we can choose which test to run, as shown in Figure 9-2.

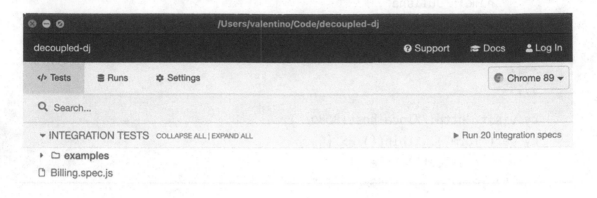

Figure 9-2. Cypress welcome page

By clicking on the spec file `Billing.spec.js`, we can run the test, but before doing so we need to start the Vue.js app. From another terminal, move into `billing/vue_spa` and run the following command:

```
npm run serve
```

Once done we can reload the test and let Cypress do the job. The test runner will go over every command in the test block, just like a real user would do. When the test finishes we should see all green, which is a sign that the test is passing. Figure 9-3 shows the test window.

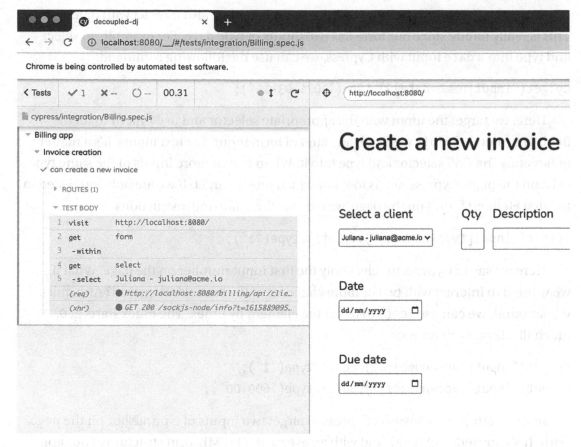

Figure 9-3. *A first passing test*

Network interception in Cypress is really convenient for working without a backend. The backend team can share the expected API request and responses with the frontend team through documentation, with actual JavaScript objects, or with JSON fixtures. On the other side, frontend developers can build the UI without having to run Django locally. In the next section we finish the test for our form by testing form inputs.

Filling and Submitting the Form

In order to submit the form, Cypress needs to fill all the required fields.

To do so, we employ a set of Cypress methods for form interaction:

- `type()` to type into input fields

- `submit()` to trigger the `submit` event on our form

With `type()` we can not only type into form fields, but also interact with date inputs. This is really handy since our form has two inputs of type `date`. For example, to select and type into a `date` input with Cypress, we can use the following command:

```
cy.get("input[name=date]").type("2021-03-15");
```

Here, we target the input with the appropriate selector and use `type()` to fill the field. This method works well with any kind of form input. For text inputs, it's a matter of targeting the CSS selector and type into it. When two or more inputs of the same type exist on the page, Cypress needs to know which one to target. If we are only interested in the first element found on the page, we can use the following instructions:

```
cy.get("input[type=number]").first().type("1");
```

Here we say to Cypress to select only the first input number on the page. What if we wanted to interact with two or more elements of the same kind instead? As a quick workaround, we can use `.eq()` to target the element by index. The index starts at 0, much like JavaScript arrays:

```
cy.get("input[type=number]").eq(0).type("1");
cy.get("input[type=number]").eq(1).type("600.00");
```

In this example, we instruct Cypress to target two inputs of type `number` on the page. With this knowledge in hand, and with an eye on the HTML form structure of our app, we can add the code shown in Listing 9-4 to our previous test.

Listing 9-4. cypress/integration/Billing.spec.js - Filling the Form with Cypress

```
...
    cy.get("form").within(() => {
      cy.get("select").select(
        "Juliana - juliana@acme.io"
      );

      cy.get("input[name=date]").type("2021-03-15");
      cy.get("input[name=due_date]").type("2021-03-30");
      cy.get("input[type=number]").eq(0).type("1");
      cy.get("input[name=description]").type(
        "Django consulting"
      );
```

```
    cy.get("input[type=number]").eq(1).type("5000.00");
  });

  cy.get("form").submit();
...
```

Here we fill all the required inputs, the two dates, the description for the invoice, and the price. Finally, we submit the form. While this test passes, Vue.js isn't that happy because it cannot route the POST request to /billing/api/invoices/. In the console, we can see the following error:

```
Proxy error: Could not proxy request /billing/api/invoices/ from
localhost:8080 to http://localhost:8000
```

This is another situation where Cypress interception can help. Before submitting the form, let's declare another interception, this time for /billing/api/invoices. Also, let's assert that the API call is triggered by the frontend; see Listing 9-5.

Listing 9-5. cypress/integration/Billing.spec.js - Adding Another Network Interception to the Test

```
...
    cy.intercept("POST", "/billing/api/invoices", {
      statusCode: 201,
      body: {},
    }).as("createInvoice");

    cy.get("form").submit();
    cy.wait("@createInvoice");
...
```

The new instructions here are as() and cy.wait(). With as(), we can alias Cypress selections, and in this case also our network intercept. With cy.wait() instead, we can wait for the network call to happen and effectively test that the frontend is making the actual API call to the backend. With this test in place we can run again Cypress, which should now give us all green, as shown in Figure 9-4.

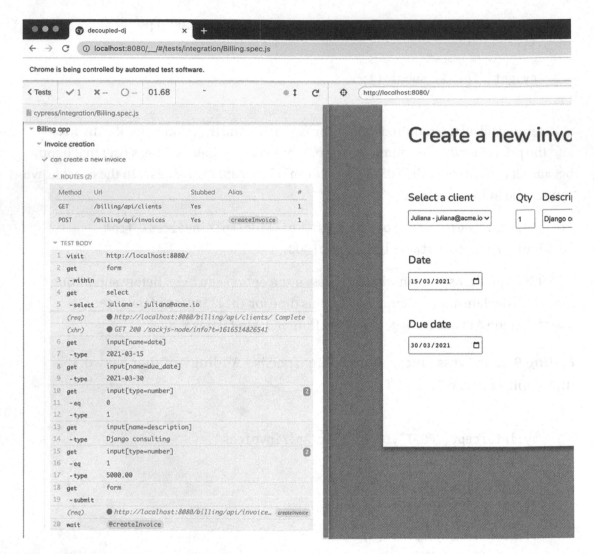

Figure 9-4. *A full test suite for our invoice form*

This concludes functional testing for the client-facing side of our app. Although limited in scope, this test helps illustrate the Cypress fundamentals. The test we wrote so far targets Vue.js without considering Django. To make our functional tests as close possible to the real world, we would also need to test the JavaScript frontend served from within Django. This is left as an exercise for the user at the end of the chapter. Let's now focus on the backend. Our REST API needs testing as well.

Introduction to Unit Testing

In contrast to functional testing, unit testing aims at ensuring that single units of code such as functions or classes work as expected.

In this chapter we don't cover unit testing for JavaScript because we already saw functional testing with Cypress, and to properly address unit testing for React and Vue.js, another chapter would not be enough. Instead, we see how to apply unit testing to the Django backend. Functional testing is an invaluable tool for checking the functionality of the UI from the user point of view. Unit testing instead ensures that our Django backend and its REST API provide the right data for our JavaScript frontend. Functional testing and unit testing are not mutually exclusive. A project should have both types of tests in place in order to be considered robust and resilient to changes. In the next section, we see how to test the Django REST Framework with Django testing tools.

Unit Testing in the Django REST Framework

Out of the box, Django makes it possible to have excellent code coverage right from the beginning. Code coverage is the measure of how much code is covered by tests. Django is a battery included framework, and it comes with a robust set of tools, like API views and a fantastic ORM, which are already tested by Django contributors and core developers. However, these tests aren't enough.

When building a project, we need to make sure that views, models, serializers, and any custom Python class or function are properly tested. Luckily, Django has us covered with a set of handy tools for unit and integration testing, like the `TestCase` class. The Django REST Framework adds some custom tooling on top of this, including:

- `APISimpleTestCase` for testing the API without database support
- `APITestCase` for testing the API along with database support

Writing a unit test for a DRF view is not so different from writing a test for a traditional Django view. The example in Listing 9-6 illustrates the minimal test structure for getting started.

Listing 9-6. Django REST Test Example

```python
from rest_framework.test import APITestCase
from rest_framework.status import HTTP_403_FORBIDDEN
from django.urls import reverse

class TestBillingAPI(APITestCase):
  @classmethod
  def setUpTestData(cls):
    pass

  def test_anon_cannot_list_clients(self):
      response = self.client.get(reverse("billing:client-list"))
      self.assertEqual(response.status_code, HTTP_403_FORBIDDEN)
```

In this example, we subclass APITestCase to declare a new test suite. Inside this class we can see a class method named setUpTestData(), which is useful for initializing data for our test. Next up we declare our first test as a class method: test_anon_cannot_list_ clients() is our first test. Inside this block, we call the API view with self.client. get(), the testing HTTP client. Then, we check that the response code we get from the view is what we expect, a 403 Forbidden in this case, since the user is not authenticated. In the next sections, we write tests for our REST views by following the example's structure.

Django Settings for Testing

Before getting started, let's configure our Django project for testing. More often than not, we will need to slightly change some setting in testing, and for this reason it is convenient to create a split setting for the testing environment. To do so, create a new file in decoupled_dj/settings/testing.py with the content shown in Listing 9-7.

Listing 9-7. decoupled_dj/settings/testing.py - Split Settings for Testing

```python
from .base import *  # noqa
```

As of now, this file doesn't do anything other than import the base settings, but this ensures that we can override any configuration if needed.

Installing the Dependencies and Configuring Requirements for Testing

We are now ready to install the dependencies for testing.

For our project, we will use two convenient libraries: `pytest` and `pytest-django`. Used together they can simplify how we run tests. For instance, when used with `pytest-django`, `pytest` can autodiscover our tests, so we don't need to add imports to our `__init__.py` files. We will also use `model-bakery`, which can ease the burden of model creation in our tests. To install these libraries, run the following command:

```
pip install pytest pytest-django model-bakery
```

Next up, create a requirements file for testing in `requirements/testing.txt` and add the lines shown in Listing 9-8.

Listing 9-8. requirements/testing.txt - Requirements for Testing

```
-r ./base.txt
model-bakery==1.2.1
pytest==6.2.2
pytest-django==4.1.0
```

This concludes our setup. We are now ready to write tests!

Outlining Tests for the Billing REST API

When writing tests, understanding what to test in a project is the most challenging task, especially for beginners.

It is easy to get lost in the testing implementation details and internal code, but really, it shouldn't be that complicated. When deciding what to test, you need to focus on one thing: the expected output from your system. In the case of our Django apps, we are exposing REST endpoints. This means we need to look at how this system is used and test these boundaries accordingly. After identifying the surface of the system, tests for the internal logic will come naturally. Let's now see what needs to be tested in our billing app. The Vue frontend from Chapter 5 invokes the following endpoints:

- `/billing/api/clients/`

- `/billing/api/invoices/`

Incidentally, these are the same endpoints that we stubbed in Cypress with `cy.intercept()`. This time we need to cover them with a unit test in Django, rather than with a functional test with Cypress. But let's step back for a moment and think about our tests. In Chapter 6, we added authentication and permissions check to our REST API. Only an authenticated admin user can invoke the API. This means we need to take authentication into account and test that we don't forget to enforce authentication by allowing anonymous users to sneak into our API. By intuition, we need to write the following tests:

- As an anonymous user, I cannot access the client list

- As an admin user, I can access the client list

- As an anonymous user, I cannot create a new invoice

- As an admin user, I can create a new invoice

Let's write these tests in the next section.

Testing the Billing REST API

To start, create a new Python package named `tests` in `billing`.

In this folder create a new file called `test_api.py`. In this file, we are going to place our test class, with the same structure we saw in the previous example. We also add all the test methods to our class, as outlined in the previous section. Listing 9-9 shows the backbone of this test.

Listing 9-9. billing/tests/test_api.py - Test Case for the Billing API

```python
from rest_framework.test import APITestCase
from rest_framework.status import HTTP_403_FORBIDDEN, HTTP_200_OK,
HTTP_201_CREATED
from django.urls import reverse

class TestBillingAPI(APITestCase):
    @classmethod
    def setUpTestData(cls):
        pass
```

```python
def test_anon_cannot_list_clients(self):
    response = self.client.get(reverse("billing:client-list"))
    self.assertEqual(response.status_code, HTTP_403_FORBIDDEN)

def test_admin_can_list_clients(self):
    # TODO: authenticate as admin
    response = self.client.get(reverse("billing:client-list"))
    self.assertEqual(response.status_code, HTTP_200_OK)

def test_anon_cannot_create_invoice(self):
    response = self.client.post(
        reverse("billing:invoice-create"), data={}, format="json"
    )
    self.assertEqual(response.status_code, HTTP_403_FORBIDDEN)
```

This test is far from being complete. Tests for the anonymous user look fine, but we can't say the same for admin because we are not authenticated in our tests yet. To create an admin user (a staff user for Django) in our tests, we can use baker() from model-bakery in setUpTestData(), and then the force_login() method on the test client, as in Listing 9-10.

Listing 9-10. billing/tests/test_api.py - Authenticating as an Admin in Our Test

```python
from rest_framework.test import APITestCase
from rest_framework.status import HTTP_403_FORBIDDEN, HTTP_200_OK,
HTTP_201_CREATED
from django.urls import reverse
from model_bakery import baker

class TestBillingAPI(APITestCase):
    @classmethod
    def setUpTestData(cls):
        cls.admin = baker.make("users.User", is_staff=True)

    def test_anon_cannot_list_clients(self):
        response = self.client.get(reverse("billing:client-list"))
        self.assertEqual(response.status_code, HTTP_403_FORBIDDEN)
```

```
def test_admin_can_list_clients(self):
    self.client.force_login(self.admin)
    response = self.client.get(reverse("billing:client-list"))
    self.assertEqual(response.status_code, HTTP_200_OK)

def test_anon_cannot_create_invoice(self):
    response = self.client.post(
        reverse("billing:invoice-create"), data={}, format="json"
    )
    self.assertEqual(response.status_code, HTTP_403_FORBIDDEN)
```

With this test in place, we are now ready to test things out. In the terminal, run the following command to switch Django to the testing environment:

```
export DJANGO_SETTINGS_MODULE=decoupled_dj.settings.testing
```

Then, run pytest:

```
pytest
```

If everything goes well, we should see the following output in the console:

```
billing/tests/test_api.py ... [100%]
============= 3 passed in 0.94s ==========
```

Our tests are passing! We can now add one last case to our test: as an admin user, I can create a new invoice. To do so, we create a new method in the class. In this method, we log in as admin and make a POST request to the API, by providing a request body. Let's not forget that, to create an invoice, we must also pass a list of item lines. This can be done in the request body. The following listing shows the complete test method, where we also create a user before the request body. This user is later associated with the invoice, as shown in Listing 9-11.

Listing 9-11. billing/tests/test_api.py - Testing Invoice Creation as an Admin

```
...
def test_admin_can_create_invoice(self):
    self.client.force_login(self.admin)
    user = baker.make("users.User")
    data = {
```

```
        "user": user.pk,
        "date": "2021-03-15",i
        "due_date": "2021-03-30",
        "items": [
            {
                "quantity": 1,
                "description": "Django consulting",
                "price": 5000.00,
                "taxed": True,
            }
        ],
    }
    response = self.client.post(
        reverse("billing:invoice-create"), data, format="json"
    )
    self.assertEqual(response.status_code, HTTP_201_CREATED)
...
```

This concludes our unit test for the billing app REST API. Alongside a functional test, we covered the whole spectrum of communication between the backend and frontend.

Note It is a good moment to commit the changes you made so far and to push the work to your Git repo. You can find the source code for this chapter at `https://github.com/valentinogagliardi/decoupled-dj/tree/chapter_09_testing`.

EXERCISE 9-1: TESTING DJANGO AND VUE.JS

Our functional test with Cypress does not take into account that Vue.js is served from a Django view in production. So far, we tested the Vue.js app in isolation. Write a functional test against the Django view that's serving the app.

EXERCISE 9-2: TESTING THE BLOG APP

Now that you learned how to structure and write tests with Cypress and Django, write a set of functional tests for the Next.js app. Write unit tests for the blog REST API as well.

Summary

Testing is often an art of intuition in identifying and covering all the possible corner cases. This chapter outlined tools and techniques for:

- Functional testing with Cypress
- Unit testing in Django, using the DRF's testing tools

In the next chapter, we move to the next big topic: authentication.

Additional Resource

- Intercepting network requests with Cypress

CHAPTER 10

Authentication and Authorization in the Django REST Framework

This chapter covers:

- Token-based authentication and JWT in brief
- Session-based authentication for single-page apps

Writing a technical book means starting with a billion topics to cover, and not enough space to fit everything in.

Authentication is one of those huge topics that almost impossible to cover deeply in a single chapter. There are simply too many scenarios: mobile applications, desktop applications, and single-page apps. Since this book has been more about single-page applications and JavaScript paired with Django, this chapter focuses only on the interaction between these two actors. In the first part, we discuss token-based authentication. In the second part, we resort to a battle-tested authentication flow, paired with single-page applications.

Note The rest of this chapter assumes you are in the repo root `decoupled-dj`, with the Python virtual environment active and with `DJANGO_SETTINGS_MODULE` configured as `decoupled_dj.settings.development`.

V. Gagliardi, *Decoupled Django*, https://doi.org/10.1007/978-1-4842-7144-5_10

Introduction to Token-Based Authentication and JWT

In Chapter 6, we created a pseudo-decoupled Django project with the DRF and Vue.js.

In Chapter 7, we hardened the security of our project, by adding a minimal form of authentication and authorization. We saw how to use session-based authentication to protect our single-page application when it's served from a Django view. In Chapter 8 we added Next.js to the mix. To generate a blog starting from our Django project, we had to disable authentication altogether. This is far from optimal and leads us to think also about all those situations where the frontend is completely decoupled from the Django backend. In a traditional setup, it is possible to use cookies and session-based authentication without much hassle. However, when the frontend and the backend are on different domains, authentication becomes tricky. Also, since sessions are stored on the server, the interchange of session cookies and CSRF cookies between the frontend and the backend violates the stateless nature of REST. For this reason, over the years, the community came up with a form of token-based authentication called *JSON Web Token*.

For authentication in decoupled setups, token-based authentication with JWT is all the rage these days, especially in the JavaScript community. In Django, JWT is not yet standardized into the core. What follows is an introduction to JWT, token-based authentication, and a discussion of their potential pitfalls.

Token-Based Authentication: The Good and the Bad

Token-based authentication is not a new concept by any means.

A token is a simple identifier that the frontend can exchange with the backend to prove that it has the rights to read or write to the backend. In the simplest arrangement, the decoupled frontend sends a username and password to the backend. On the other side, the backend verifies the user's credentials, and if they are valid, it sends a token back to the frontend. The token is usually a simple alphanumeric string, such as the following example:

```
9944b09199c62bcf9418ad846dd0e4bbdfc6ee4b
```

When the frontend wants to make requests to a protected resource on the API, be it a GET or a POST request, it has to send back this token by including it in the request headers. The Django REST Framework has out-of-the-box support for token-based authentication with the TokenAuthentication scheme.

In terms of security, this authentication mechanism is far from being bulletproof. First off, sending the credentials over the wire, namely a username and password, is not the best approach, even under HTTPS. Also, once we obtain a token in the frontend, we need to persist it during the entire user session, and sometimes even beyond that. To persist the token, most developers resort to saving it in `localStorage`, a huge mistake which effectively opens the application to a whole new set of risks. `localStorage` is vulnerable to XSS attacks, where an attacker injects malicious JavaScript code in a web page it has control of, lures the user to visit it, and steals any non `HttpOnly` cookies, as well as potentially any data saved in `localStorage`.

In terms of the capabilities of these tokens instead, they are very simple. They do not carry info about the user, nor indications on what permissions the user has. They are strictly tied to Django and to its database, and only Django can pair a given user with its token. Their simplicity is a "feature" of these basic tokens. Despite these limitations, token-based authentication works well in all those situations where the frontend is on a different domain from the backend. However, over the years, the JavaScript community has pondered about the opportunity to create more structured tokens. This led to the creation of a new standard called JSON Web Tokens, which introduced innovations as well as more challenges.

JSON Web Tokens in Django: Advantages and Challenges

A JSON Web Token, or JWT for short, is a standard that defines a convenient way to exchange authentication information between a client and a server.

JWT tokens are a completely different beast from a simple alphanumeric token. First off, they are signed. That is, they are encrypted by the server before being sent off the wire and are decrypted back on the client. This is necessary because JWT tokens contain sensitive information that can be used to authenticate against protected resources if these tokens are stolen. JWT has a solid market share in the JavaScript/Node.js community.

On the Django scene instead, they are considered an insecure authentication method. The reason for this is that server-side JWT implementations are hard to get right, and there are simply too many things in the spec left open to interpretation for the implementer, which can build an insecure JWT server without even knowing. To learn more about all the security implications of JWT, check out the first link in the additional resources. In brief, as of today, Django has no core support for JWT, and this situation is not going to change in the future.

If you want to use JWT in your own Django projects, a number of libraries exist, like `django-rest-framework-simplejwt`. This library does not handle the registration flow, but only the issuing phase of JWT. In other words, from the frontend we can use `api/token/` and `api/token/refresh/` with the username and password to request a new token or refresh a token if we have a token in hand. When a client requests a token from the server, the server replies with two tokens: an access token and a refresh token. Access tokens usually have an expiration date as a security measure. Refresh tokens, on the other hand, are used by the client to request a new access token when the latter expires. The access token is used for authentication, and the refresh token is used for requesting a new authentication token. Since both tokens are equally important, they must be both protected adequately on the client.

As with any token, JWT tokens are often subject to the same pitfalls. Most developers persist JWT tokens in `localStorage`, which is vulnerable to XSS. This is possibly even worse than persisting a simple alphanumeric token, as JWT carries much more sensitive information in its body, and even if it's encrypted, we can't be lax about protecting it. To avoid these risks, developers resort to saving JWT tokens in `HttpOnly` cookies, which coincidentally sounds a lot like the most classic session-based authentication method. In the end, even if JWT tokens are convenient for cross-domain and mobile authentication, maintaining such an infrastructure can be hard and prone to security risks. Is there an easy path to authentication with Django and single-page applications? we'll explore that question in the next sections.

Session-Based Auth for Single-Page Apps

In the end, authentication for Django projects should not be complicated, at least for web apps.

In fact, with the help of NGINX, we can use session-based authentication instead of tokens, even for single-page apps. In Chapter 7 we deployed our Django app with a traditional setup, which was a Django template serving a single-page application. What if we turn things upside down now, by serving a single-page application as the main entry point to our Django project? There are a few steps we need to think about before this can happen. In particular, NGINX should:

- Serve a single-page app from the root location block

- Proxy API, auth, and admin requests to Django

To do this, we need to make the necessary adjustments to the configuration from Chapter 7. Let's see what needs to be done in the next sections.

Note   The configuration we are going to see is completely independent of the one in Chapter 7. They are two different approaches, both valid.

Some Words on Production and Development

The scenario provided in the following sections is not easily replicable on the local workstation, unless you're using Docker or a virtual machine.

To keep things as close as possible to reality, we present a production environment where the application is deployed at https://decoupled-django.com/, with a valid SSL certificate. If you want to replicate the same environment, you have two options:

- Use Docker to run NGINX, Django, and Vue.js (not covered in this book).

- Use a virtual machine environment, such as VirtualBox, to create a Linux machine and then run the Ansible playbook from https:// github.com/valentinogagliardi/decoupled-dj/tree/chapter_10_ authentication.

If you go with the second option, here are some tips:

- In the VirtualBox instance, forward a port for SSH and another for the web server, from the guest to the host. For SSH you can pick 8022 for the guest, forwarded to 22 on the host, and for the web server, pick port 80 forwarded from the guest to the host.

- In the /etc/hosts file of your main workstation, configure the decoupled-django.com domain and the static.decoupled-django.com subdomain to point to 127.0.0.1.

With the virtual machine in place, from your workstation, run the Ansible playbook with the following command:

```
ansible-playbook -i deployment/inventory deployment/site.yml --extra-vars
"trustme=yes"
```

This playbook will configure the environment, deploy the code, and create a fake SSL certificate for `decoupled-django.com` and `static.decoupled-django.com`. Once it's done, you can access `https://decoupled-django.com/` in your browser, after adding an exception for the certificates.

Note   Instructions on how to run the playbook can be found at `https://github.com/valentinogagliardi/decoupled-dj/blob/chapter_10_authentication/README.md#deployment`.

Preparing NGINX for the New Setup

As a first step, we need to configure NGINX to serve our single-page application on the root `location` block.

Listing 10-1 shows the first change.

Listing 10-1. deployment/templates/decoupled-django.com.j2 - NGINX Configuration to Serve the Single-Page Application

```
...
location / {
    alias /home/{{ user }}/code/billing/vue_spa/dist/;
}
...
```

This is different from what we saw in Chapter 7, where the main entry point of the project was Gunicorn. In this example, we reuse the Vue.js single-page app from Chapter 6, which is a simple form for creating invoices, but to test things out, we promote it to the main single-page app for our project. Here we say to NGINX, when a user visits the root of our website, send it to the Vue.js app in `/home/decoupled-django/code/billing/vue_spa/dist/`. What is `dist` here? By default, Vue CLI builds the production JS bundle in the `dist` folder of the Vue.js project. This is the default configuration, but in Chapter 6 we changed it to emit the bundles where Django would expect them, in static files. Now we go back to the default. To make this work, we also need to tweak Vue.js a bit in a moment. With this configuration, by visiting `https://decoupled-django.com/` in production, NGINX will serve the single-page app. However, as soon as Vue.js loads, it makes a call to `billing/api/clients/` to fetch a list of clients for the `<select>`. This leads us to adjust the NGINX configuration again so that any request to `/api/` is proxied to Gunicorn, and thus to Django. Listing 10-2 shows the additional NGINX block.

Listing 10-2. deployment/templates/decoupled-django.com.j2 - NGINX Configuration to Proxy API Requests to Django

```
location ~* /api/ {
    proxy_pass http://gunicorn;
    proxy_set_header Host $host;
    proxy_set_header X-Real-IP $remote_addr;
    proxy_set_header X-Forwarded-For $proxy_add_x_forwarded_for;
    proxy_set_header X-Forwarded-Proto $scheme;
}
```

With this change in place, API calls will actually reach Django. There's still one detail missing: authentication. Everything changes with this setup. Django is not in charge of serving the single-page app anymore, but it should indeed serve the API and the login flow, for a good reason—more on this in the next section.

Handling the Login Flow with Django

We want to use a single-page application as the main entry point to our Django project, but we also want to use session-based authentication from Django.

This is the point where we hit a conundrum. How do we authenticate our users without involving tokens? Django has a built-in authentication system, part of the `contrib` module, from which we can peruse a set of views for handling the most common authentication flows: login/logout, register/confirm, and password reset. For example, `LoginView` from `django.contrib.auth.views` can help with the login flow. However, the problem with our current setup is that the single-page application is now completely decoupled from the Django project.

As a naive approach, we could try to make a `POST` request to a Django `LoginView` from JavaScript, but these views are protected with a CSRF check. This is the same problem we hit before, but now it is more serious because we don't have any Django view from which we can grab the CSRF token before issuing the request. The solution?

We can let Django handle the authentication flow. To do so, we are going to create a standalone Django application for the authentication logic. In the root project folder, run the following command:

```
python manage.py startapp login
```

Next, create a new URL configuration in login/urls.py and place the code shown in Listing 10-3 inside it.

Listing 10-3. login/urls.py - URL Configuration for Login and Logout Views

```
from django.urls import path
from django.contrib.auth.views import LoginView, LogoutView

app_name = "auth"

urlpatterns = [
    path(
        "login/",
        LoginView.as_view(
            template_name="login/login.html",
            redirect_authenticated_user=True
        ),
        name="login",
    ),
    path("logout/", LogoutView.as_view(), name="logout"),
]
```

Here we declare two routes, one for login and another for logout. The LoginView uses a custom template_name. Create the template in login/templates/login/login.html, as shown in Listing 10-4.

Listing 10-4. login/templates/login/login.html - Login Form

```
<!DOCTYPE html>
<html lang="en">
<head>
    <meta charset="UTF-8">
    <title>Login</title>
</head>
```

```html
<body>
<form method="POST" action="{% url "auth:login" %}">
    {% csrf_token %}
    <div>
        <label for="{{ form.username.id_for_label }}">Username:</label>
        <input type="text" name="username" autofocus maxlength="254"
        required id="id_username">
    </div>
    <div>
        <label for="{{ form.password.id_for_password }}">Password:</label>
        <input type="password" name="password" autocomplete="current-
        password" required="" id="id_password">
    </div>
    <input type="hidden" name="next" value="{{ next }}">
    <button type="submit" value="login">
        LOGIN
    </button>
</form>
{{ form.non_field_errors }}
</body>
</html>
```

This is a simple HTML form augmented with Django template tags; specifically, it includes {% csrf_token %}. When the form is rendered, Django places a hidden HTML input in the markup, as shown in Listing 10-5.

Listing 10-5. Django's CSRF Token in HTML Forms

```html
<input type="hidden" name="csrfmiddlewaretoken" value="2TYg60oCOGC2LW7oJEPw
Bsg2ajZsjJOn5Wvjqd28J9wMcGBanbnNfkmfT5Qw3juK">
```

The value of this input is sent alongside POST requests to Django LoginView. If the user's credentials are valid, Django redirects the user to a URL of choice, and sends two cookies to the browser: csrftoken and sessionid. To make this work, we need to load the login app and configure the redirect URL in decoupled_dj/settings/base.py, as shown in Listing 10-6.

Listing 10-6. decoupled_dj/settings/base.py - Enabling the Login App and Configuring the Login Redirect URL

```
INSTALLED_APPS = [
    ...
    "login"
]

...

LOGIN_REDIRECT_URL = "/"
```

Once this is done, include the new URLs in the root configuration, decoupled_dj/ urls.py, as shown in Listing 10-7.

Listing 10-7. decoupled_dj/urls.py - Including the URL from the Login App

```
urlpatterns = [
    ...
    path("auth/", include("login.urls", namespace="auth")),
]
```

As a last step, we tell NGINX that any request to /auth/ must be proxied to Django, as shown in Listing 10-8.

Listing 10-8. deployment/templates/decoupled-django.com.j2 - NGINX Configuration to Proxy Authentication Requests to Django

```
location /auth/ {
    proxy_pass http://gunicorn;
    proxy_set_header Host $host;
    proxy_set_header X-Real-IP $remote_addr;
    proxy_set_header X-Forwarded-For $proxy_add_x_forwarded_for;
    proxy_set_header X-Forwarded-Proto $scheme;
}
```

What do we achieve with this setup? NGINX now replies as follows:

- Requests to `https://decoupled-django.com/auth/login/` are proxied to Gunicorn/Django

- Requests to `https://decoupled-django.com/` are proxied to Vue.js

- Requests to `https://decoupled-django.com/billing/api/` are proxied to Gunicorn/Django

In this arrangement, Django handles the whole authentication flow with session-based authentication. On the other hand, the single-page application merely makes API calls to Django. In this regard, we need to fix Vue.js to work with the new setup.

Note   You can find the source code for the NGINX configuration at `https://github.com/valentinogagliardi/decoupled-dj/tree/chapter_10_authentication/deployment/templates/`.

Preparing the Vue.js App for the New Setup

To recap, in Chapter 6 we configured `vue.config.js` and `.env.staging` to make Django static files work with Vue.js.

In Chapter 7 we added another piece to the puzzle, by configuring `.env.production` so that Vue.js could recognize the subdomain from where it was loaded. In this chapter, we can get rid of those configurations. The configuration files `vue.config.js`, `.env.staging`, and `.env.production` can be removed from `billing/vue_spa/`. By doing so, when building the production bundle, the JavaScript files and assets will land in the `dist` folder. This folder is usually excluded from the source control, so we need to install Node.js on the target machine to install JavaScript dependencies and build the bundle from `/home/decoupled-django/code/billing/vue_spa`. Once this is done, we can run our Vue.js app as the main entry point to the Django project.

Note   The Ansible playbook at `https://github.com/valentinogagliardi/decoupled-dj/tree/chapter_10_authentication` takes care of installing Node.js and building the bundle.

The effect of this setup is that the JavaScript frontend will pass cookies to Django without any intervention from us. Figure 10-1 shows `csrftoken` and `sessionid` travelling with the `GET` request to `/billing/api/clients`.

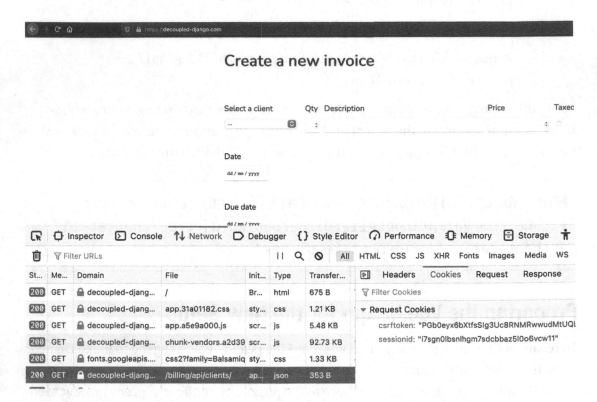

Figure 10-1. *GET requests from JavaScript to Django include the session cookie and the CSRF token*

Figure 10-2 shows the same cookies, this time transmitted with a `POST` request.

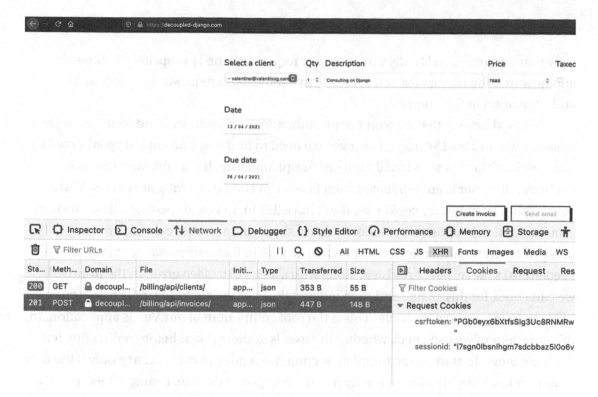

Figure 10-2. *POST requests from JavaScript to Django include the session cookie and the CSRF token*

There isn't anything magical in this setup: cookies can travel on the same origin, even over Fetch.

A Note About HttpOnly Cookies

An HttpOnly cookie is a cookie that can't be read from JavaScript code.

By default, Django already ensures that sessionid has the HttpOnly attribute. This doesn't break cookie exchange with fetch because the same-origin default behavior ensures that cookies are sent back and forth when the calling JavaScript code has the same origin of the targeted URL. As for csrftoken, we need to leave it accessible to JavaScript because we include it as a header alongside non-safe HTTP requests (POST and the like).

Handling Authentication in the Frontend

Now that we configured NGINX to proxy our requests to the appropriate destination, and now that the Django backend is ready to handle login requests, we can handle authentication in the frontend.

The good news is that we won't write authentication forms by hand, send out tokens, or save them in `localStorage`. However, we need to find a way around `HttpOnly` cookies, since we can't access `sessionid` from JavaScript anymore. It is a common practice to check if the user is authenticated from JavaScript code by looking at cookies. With `sessionid` as a `HttpOnly` cookie, we don't have this luxury (and relaxing this protection is not an option). A possible solution hides in the error messages coming from our REST API. Any unauthenticated request to the DRF in fact returns `Authentication credentials were not provided`, along with a `403 Forbidden` error. In the frontend, we can check for this signal, and then redirect the user to `/auth/login/`. Let's open `billing/vue_spa/src/App.vue`. This is the root component of our Vue.js application. In this component we can check whether the user is authenticated before redirecting it to the login view. To start, in the template section, we render `InvoiceCreate` only if the user is authenticated by checking a Boolean in the component's state. Listing 10-9 shows the changes in the `<template>` section.

Listing 10-9. billing/vue_spa/src/App.vue - Checking if the User Is Logged In

```
<template>
 <div id="app">
   <div v-if="isLoggedIn">
     <InvoiceCreate />
   </div>
   <div v-else></div>
 </div>
</template>
```

In the script section of the component, we assemble the following logic:

- In `mounted()`, we make a call to an endpoint
- If we get a `200`, we consider the user authenticated
- If we get a `Forbidden`, we jump to check the exact type of error from the Django REST Framework

Listing 10-10 shows the changes in the `<script>` section.

Listing 10-10. billing/vue_spa/src/App.vue - Handling Authentication in the Frontend

```
<template>
 <div id="app">
   <div v-if="isLoggedIn">
     <InvoiceCreate />
   </div>
   <div v-else></div>
 </div>
</template>

<script>
import InvoiceCreate from "@/components/InvoiceCreate";

export default {
 name: "App",
 components: {
   InvoiceCreate
 },
 data: function() {
   return {
     isLoggedIn: false
   };
 },
 methods: {
   redirectToLogin: function() {
     this.isLoggedIn = false;
     window.location.href = "/auth/login/";
   }
 },
 mounted() {
   fetch("/billing/api/clients/")
     .then(response => {
```

```
      if (
        !response.ok &&
        response.statusText === "Forbidden"
      ) {
        return response.json();
      }
      this.isLoggedIn = true;
    })
    .then(drfError => {
      switch (drfError?.detail) {
        case "Authentication credentials were not provided.":
          this.redirectToLogin();
          break;
        default:
          break;
      }
    });
  }
};
</script>
```

In this code, we make an AJAX request to an endpoint of choice. If the request returns a `Forbidden`, we check what kind of error the Django REST Framework gives us, with a simple `switch` statement. The first error message we may want to check for is `Authentication credentials were not provided.` This is a clear sign that we are trying to access a protected resource without credentials. If you are worried that checking authentication or permissions by the means of strings will look hacky because Django could sooner or later change the error message and return an unexpected string, in my experience there is always some kind of contract between frontend and backend developers to agree on which response bodies or error messages they can expect from each other. If strings are a concern, these can be easily abstracted away into constants. Not counting that the frontend and the backend must always be put under a strong test suite.

Note   In this example, we use `fetch()` to avoid pulling in additional dependencies. Another valid alternative is `axios`, which has a convenient interceptor feature.

With this logic in place, we can add more checks, such as permissions, as we will see in the next section. This isn't the most clever implementation, but it gets the job done, and more important, it uses a battle-tested authentication method. The same approach can also be used with React: we can serve the single-page application from NGINX, with Django lurking in the background. It is important to note that this setup works only when Django and the single-page are served under the same domain. This is easily achievable with NGINX and Docker. For all those configurations where the client lives on a different domain instead, token-based authentication is required. With the authentication part in place, let's now explore authorization in the Django REST Framework.

Note   In the previous example, we used `window.location` to redirect the user. If you use Vue router, the code must be adjusted to use `this.$router.push()`.

Authorization and Permissions in the Django REST Framework

Once a user logs in, we are in the middle of the flow.

Authentication is the "who are you" part of the whole story. Next comes the "what can you do" part. In Chapter 7, we locked down our API by allowing access only to admin users. Listing 10-11 shows the configuration applied in `decoupled_dj/settings/base.py`.

Listing 10-11. decoupled_dj/setting/base.py - Adding Permissions Globally in the DRF

```
REST_FRAMEWORK = {
  "DEFAULT_AUTHENTICATION_CLASSES": [
      "rest_framework.authentication.SessionAuthentication",
  ],
```

```
"DEFAULT_PERMISSION_CLASSES": [
    "rest_framework.permissions.IsAdminUser"
],
}
```

To test things in the frontend, we can create an unprivileged user in our Django project. Open a Django shell and run the following ORM instruction:

```
User.objects.create_user(username="regular-user", password="insecure-pass")
```

This will create a new user in the database. If we try to log in with this user on auth/ login/, Django will redirect back to the homepage as expected, but once we land there, we won't see anything in the interface. This is because our JavaScript frontend isn't wired to handle the case where the Django REST Framework responds with You do not have permission to perform this action. We can see this error in the Network tab of the browser's console for the call to billing/api/clients. With DRF permissions, we can give users access to REST views. Permissions can be not only set at the configuration level, but also with granularity on each view. To permit access to authenticated users, not only to admin on billing/api/clients, we can use the IsAuthenticated permission class. To apply this permission, open billing/api/views.py and adjust the code as shown in Listing 10-12.

Listing 10-12. billing/api/views.py - Applying Permissions on the View Level

```
...
from rest_framework.permissions import IsAuthenticated

class ClientList(ListAPIView):
    permission_classes = [IsAuthenticated]

    serializer_class = UserSerializer
    queryset = User.objects.all()
...
```

With this change, any authenticated user can access the view. In the frontend, we can handle permissions errors by adding another check in the switch statement, which looks for You do not have permission to perform this action in the response from the API and shows a user-friendly message to our users. Of course, the permission story does not stop here. In the Django REST Framework, we can customize permissions, grant permissions on the object level, and much more. The documentation covers almost every possible use case.

Note   It is a good moment to commit the changes you made so far and to push the work to your Git repo. You can find the source code for this chapter at `https://github.com/valentinogagliardi/decoupled-dj/tree/chapter_10_authentication`.

Summary

You learned some important key takeaways from this chapter:

- Never store tokens or other sensitive data in `localStorage`

- Whenever possible, use session-based authentication to secure single-page apps

In the next chapter, we begin our exploration of GraphQL in Django with Ariadne.

Additional Resource

- JWTs in Django

CHAPTER 11

GraphQL in Django with Ariadne

This chapter covers:

- GraphQL schema, operations, and resolvers
- Ariadne in Django
- React and Django with GraphQL

In the first part of this chapter, we augment the billing app from Chapter 6 with a GraphQL API. Later, we begin to connect a React/TypeScript frontend to the GraphQL backend.

Note   This chapter assumes you are in the repo root `decoupled-dj`, with the Python virtual environment active and with `DJANGO_SETTINGS_MODULE` configured as `decoupled_dj.settings.development`.

Getting Started with Ariadne in Django

Chapter 1 covered the fundamentals of GraphQL.

We learned that in order to get data from a GraphQL API, we send a query over a POST request. To change data on the database instead, we send a so-called *mutation*. It's now time to put the theory in practice by introducing GraphQL into our Django project with Ariadne, a GraphQL library for Python. Ariadne uses a schema-first approach. In schema-first, the GraphQL API gets shaped with the GraphQL Schema Definition Language, in the form of a string or a `.graphql` file.

© Valentino Gagliardi 2021
V. Gagliardi, *Decoupled Django*, https://doi.org/10.1007/978-1-4842-7144-5_11

Installing Ariadne

To start off, we install Ariadne in the Django project:

```
pip install ariadne
```

After the installation, we update `requirements/base.txt` to include the new dependency. Next, we enable Ariadne in `decoupled_dj/settings/base.py`, as shown in Listing 11-1.

Listing 11-1. decoupled_dj/settings/base.py - Enabling Ariadne in INSTALLED_APPS

```
INSTALLED_APPS = [
    ...
    "ariadne.contrib.django",
]
```

We also need to make sure that `APP_DIRS` in `TEMPLATES` is set to `True`, as shown in Listing 11-2.

Listing 11-2. decoupled_dj/settings/base.py - Template Configuration

```
TEMPLATES = [
    {
    ...
    "APP_DIRS": True,
    ...
]
```

That's all we need to do to get started. After enabling Ariadne, we are now ready to start building our GraphQL schema.

Designing the GraphQL Schema

GraphQL enforces the Schema Definition Language to define a schema, which is the principal building block for the GraphQL API.

This is a large departure from REST where the backend code usually comes first, and only later we generate documentation for the API. This concept in GraphQL is turned upside down: we create the schema first, which acts both as a documentation and as a contract between the GraphQL API and its consumers. Without a schema we cannot send queries or mutations to the GraphQL API: we would get an error, because the schema drives exactly what the consumer can ask the service. What's in a schema? The GraphQL schema contains a definition of all the operations and model entities available for consumers. Before thinking about our schema, let's recap the entities involved in our billing app. We have the following endpoints:

- `/billing/api/clients/`
- `/billing/api/invoices/`

Plus, we have the following models:

- `User`
- `Invoice`, connected with a foreign key to `User`
- `ItemLine`, connected with a foreign key to `Invoice`

Our GraphQL schema must contain the shape of all these models (as long as we want to expose them in the API), plus the shape of each permitted GraphQL operation, with their return values. What does this mean in practice? In order to send a `getClients` query to the GraphQL API, we first need to define its shape in the schema. Take for example the query in Listing 11-3.

Listing 11-3. Example of a Typical GraphQL Query

```
query {
  getClients {
      name
  }
}
```

Without the corresponding schema, the query would fail with the following error:

```
Cannot query field 'getClients' on type 'Query'
```

All the queries, mutations, and subscriptions available in the GraphQL schema go under the name of *operations*.

With this knowledge, let's define our first schema. Create a new file at `billing/schema.graphql`. Notice it has a `.graphql` extension. Most editors and IDEs offer completion and IntelliSense for the language, thus it makes sense to have the schema in its own file. As an alternative we could also write the schema directly as a triple-quoted string in the code. In this example, we take the first approach. In the schema we are going to define all the entities for the billing app, plus a first query for getting all clients from the database. Where do we get the shape of our objects? Since our app already has a REST API with the DRF, we can look at `billing/api/serializers.py` to see what fields are exposed there. After all, DRF serializers are the public interface between Django models and the rest of the world, and so it's the GraphQL schema in its own way. Also, we should look in `billing/models.py` to see how our models are connected, in order to express the same relationships in GraphQL. Listing 11-4 shows our first schema based on our models and on the appropriate fields defined in DRF serializers.

Listing 11-4. billing/schema.graphql - First Iteration of the GraphQL Schema for the Billing App

```
enum InvoiceState {
    PAID
    UNPAID
    CANCELLED
}

type User {
    id: ID
    name: String
    email: String
}

type Invoice {
    user: User
    date: String
    dueDate: String
    state: InvoiceState
    items: [ItemLine]
}

type ItemLine {
```

```
    quantity: Int
    description: String
    price: Float
    taxed: Boolean
}

type Query {
    getClients: [User]
}
```

From the schema we can immediately recognize GraphQL scalar types: ID, String, Boolean, Int, and Float. These types describe what type of data each field of the object has. We can also notice an enum type, which represents the different states of an Invoice. In our serializer we didn't expose the state field for an Invoice, but it is a good time to include it in the GraphQL schema. As for the model entities in our database, notice User, Invoice, and ItemLine as custom objects types with fields. Another thing that stands out is the way in which model relationships are described. From top to bottom, we can see that:

- Invoice as a user field to a User

- Invoice as an items field to a list of ItemLines

- The getClients query resolves (returns) a list of Users

Really, the schema is expressiveness at its finest. It's also worth noting that this schema isn't perfect yet, for many reasons. For example, Invoice has date and dueDate represented as String. This is not what Django expects. We will fix these inconsistencies later. Eager to see what a GraphQL API looks like in Django, in the next section we load the schema in Ariadne.

Loading the Schema in Ariadne

We are a couple of steps away from setting up our first GraphQL endpoint in Django.

To do so, we need to load the schema and make it executable. Create another file at billing/schema.py, which should contain the code in Listing 11-5.

Listing 11-5. billing/schema.py - Loading the Schema in Ariadne

```python
from ariadne import load_schema_from_path, gql, make_executable_schema
from ariadne import ObjectType
from pathlib import Path

BASE_DIR = Path(__file__).resolve().parent

schema_file = load_schema_from_path(BASE_DIR / "schema.graphql")
type_defs = gql(schema_file)

query = ObjectType("Query")

"""
TODO: Write resolvers
"""

schema = make_executable_schema(type_defs, query)
```

In this snippet, we import the necessary tools from Ariadne. In particular:

- load_schema_from_path loads our schema file from the filesystem

- gql validates the schema

- ObjectType creates root types (Query, Mutation, and Subscription)

- make_executable_schema connects the schema to *resolvers*, Python functions that execute queries against the database

In this first snippet we don't have any resolver yet. We will add some in the next sections. It's also important to note that this code does not do anything on the database yet. In the next section, we wire up billing/schema.py to a Django URL.

Wiring Up the GraphQL Endpoint

Before making queries to the GraphQL API, we need to connect our schema to a Django URL.

To do so, we add an URL named graphql/ in billing/urls.py, as shown in Listing 11-6.

Listing 11-6. billing/urls.py - Enabling the GraphQL Endpoint

```python
from django.urls import path
from .views import Index
from .api.views import ClientList, InvoiceCreate
from ariadne.contrib.django.views import GraphQLView
from .schema import schema

app_name = "billing"

urlpatterns = [
    path("", Index.as_view(), name="index"),
    path("api/clients/", ClientList.as_view(), name="client-list"),
    path("api/invoices/", InvoiceCreate.as_view(), name="invoice-create"),
    path("graphql/", GraphQLView.as_view(schema=schema), name="graphql"),
]
```

In this URL configuration for Django, we import `GraphQLView` from Ariadne, which works much like a regular CBV. After saving the file and starting the Django project with `python manage.py runserver`, we can head over to `http://127.0.0.1:8000/billing/graphql/`. This should open the GraphQL Playground, an interactive tool for exploring the GraphQL API. In the playground we can send out queries, mutations, or just explore the schema and the integrated documentation. Figure 11-1 shows the schema we created before as it appears on the GraphQL Playground.

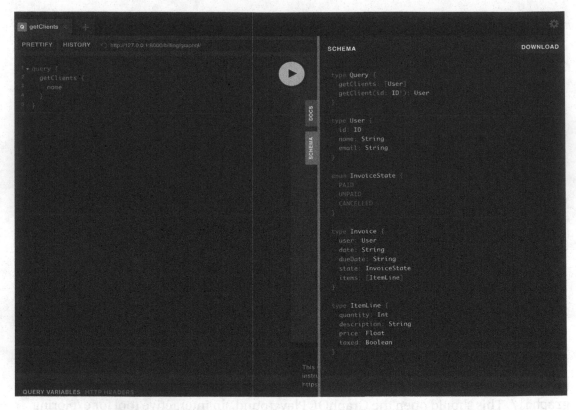

Figure 11-1. *The GraphQL Playground for Ariadne. It exposes the schema and a convenient documentation*

Figure 11-2 instead shows the auto-generated documentation for our first query.

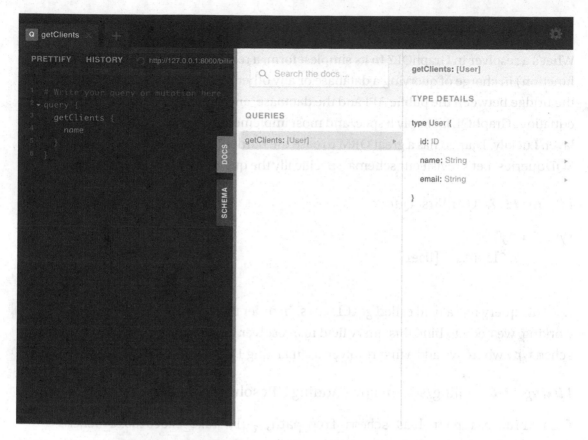

Figure 11-2. *Our first query appears in the auto-generated documentation*

To send queries to this GraphQL endpoint, we can use the playground or more realistically a JavaScript client. For a quick test, you can also use `curl`. Open another terminal and launch the following command:

```
curl -X POST --location "http://127.0.0.1:8000/billing/graphql/" \
    -H "Accept: application/json" \
    -H "Content-Type: application/json" \
    -d "{
    \"query\": \"query { getClients { name } }\"
    }"
```

In response, you should get the following result:

```
{"data": {"getClients": null } }
```

This is a sign that our GraphQL API is working, but nothing gets returned from our query. Time to meet resolvers in the next section.

181

Working with Resolvers

What's a resolver in GraphQL? In its simplest form, a resolver is a *callable* (a method or a function) in charge of querying a database or any other source. Resolvers in GraphQL are the bridge between the public API and the database, and this is also the hardest part of the equation. GraphQL is simply a spec, and most implementations do not include a database layer. Luckily, Django has a great ORM to ease the burden of working directly with raw SQL queries. Let's revisit our schema, specifically the query shown in Listing 11-7.

Listing 11-7. Our First Query

```
type Query {
    getClients: [User]
}
```

This query has a field called `getClients`. In order to get our `getClients` query working, we need to bind this query field to a resolver. To do so, we go back to `billing/schema.py` where we add a first resolver, as in Listing 11-8.

Listing 11-8. billing/schema.py - Adding a Resolver to the Mix

```
from ariadne import load_schema_from_path, gql, make_executable_schema
from ariadne import ObjectType
from pathlib import Path
from users.models import User

BASE_DIR = Path(__file__).resolve().parent

schema_file = load_schema_from_path(BASE_DIR / "schema.graphql")
type_defs = gql(schema_file)

query = ObjectType("Query")

@query.field("getClients")
def resolve_clients(obj, info):
    return User.objects.all()

schema = make_executable_schema(type_defs, query)
```

The most notable change in this file is that we import the `User` model, and we decorate a resolver function with `@query.field()`. In the example, the resolver `resolve_clients()` gets two parameters: `obj` and `info`. `info` contains details about the requested field, and more important, it carries a context object that has the HTTP request attached. This is an instance of `WSGIRequest` for a Django project running synchronously. `obj` is any value returned from a parent resolver, since resolvers can also be nested. In our example we don't use these parameters for now. Once we save the file, we can include as many fields as we want in our query for each single user. For example, we can send the query in Listing 11-9 in the GraphQL Playground.

Listing 11-9. A GraphQL Query for Fetching All Clients

```
query {
  getClients {
      id
      name
      email
  }
}
```

Notice that in the Python code for Ariadne, we didn't define resolvers for `id`, `name`, or `email`. We simply defined a resolver for the `getClients` query. It would be impractical to define by hand a resolver for each field, and luckily, GraphQL has us covered. Ariadne can handle these fields with the concept of default resolvers, taken from `graphql-core`, which Ariadne builds upon. Our query will now return the response shown in Listing 11-10.

Listing 11-10. The Response from the GraphQL API

```
{
    "data": {
        "getClients": [
            {
                "id": "1",
                "name": "Juliana",
                "email": "juliana@acme.io"
            },
```

```
            {
                "id": "2",
                "name": "John",
                "email": "john@zyx.dev"
            }
        ]
    }
}
```

If you don't have a user in the database yet, create some from the shell:

```
python manage.py shell_plus
```

To create two users, run the following queries (>>> is the shell prompt):

```
>>> User.objects.create_user(username="jul81", name="Juliana",
email="juliana@acme.io")
>>> User.objects.create_user(username="john89", name="John",
email="john@zyx.dev")
```

Note   So far we talked about databases, but GraphQL can work with almost any data source. Gatsby is a great example of this capability: the Markdown plugin for example can resolve data from .md files.

Congratulations on creating your first GraphQL endpoint! Let's now learn about query arguments in GraphQL.

Using Query Arguments in GraphQL

So far we fetched all the users from the database.

What if we want to fetch just one? This is where query arguments come into play. Let's imagine the following GraphQL query:

```
query {
 getClient(id: 2) {
   name
   email
 }
}
```

Here we have a query field, used much like a function. id is the argument for the "function". In the body instead, we declare the fields we want to fetch for the single user. To support this query, the schema must know about it. This means we need to:

- Define the new query field in the schema

- Create a resolver to fulfill the field

First off, in billing/schema.graphql, we add the new field to the existing Query object, as shown in Listing 11-11 (all the existing object types must be left intact).

Listing 11-11. billing/schema.graphql - Adding a New Field to the Query

```
type Query {
   getClients: [User]
   getClient(id: ID!): User
}
```

In the new getClient field, notice the id parameter with its scalar type ID, which is now followed by an exclamation mark. This symbol means that the parameter is non-nullable: we cannot query with a null ID, for obvious reasons.

Note   The non-nullable constraint can be applied to any GraphQL object field or list.

With the schema in good shape, we now proceed to define the new resolver in billing/schema.py, as shown in Listing 11-12 (for brevity, we show just the new resolver).

Listing 11-12. billing/schema.py - An Additional Resolver for Fulfilling the New Query

```
...
@query.field("getClient")
def resolve_client(obj, info, id):
   return User.objects.get(id=id)
...
```

In this new resolver, alongside `obj` and `info`, we can also see a third parameter named `id`. This parameter will be passed by our GraphQL query to the resolver. In general, any number of parameters defined in the query are passed down to the corresponding resolver. We can now issue the query shown in Listing 11-13 in the playground.

Listing 11-13. Retrieving a Single User from the GraphQL Playground

```
query {
 getClient(id: 2) {
   name
   email
 }
}
```

The server should return the response shown in Listing 11-14.

Listing 11-14. The GraphQL Response for a Single User

```
{
 "data": {
   "getClient": {
     "name": "John",
     "email": "john@zyx.dev"
   }
 }
}
```

After this tour of data fetching, it's now time to do something more challenging: add data with a mutation.

A Word on Schema-First vs Code-First

We can already spot a pattern after adding a couple of queries and resolvers to our GraphQL API.

Every time we need a new field, we update two files:

- `billing/schema.graphql`
- `billing/schema.py`

A solution to this problem consists in co-locating the textual schema right inside the code. Consider the following example:

```
type_defs = gql(
    """
    type User {
        id: ID
        name: String
        email: String
    }
    """
)
```

Instead of loading the schema from the file, we place it directly in `gql`. This is a convenient approach. However, the ability to derive and generate the schema starting from the code, with a code-first approach, turns out to be even more flexible than dealing with strings. Graphene and Strawberry follow this path exactly.

Implementing Mutations

Mutations in GraphQL are side effects, that is, operations meant to change the state of the database.

In Chapter 6, we worked on a REST backend, which accepted POST requests from the frontend to create new invoices. To create a new invoice, our backend wanted:

- The user ID to associate to the invoice
- The invoice date
- The invoice due date
- One or more item lines (an array) to associate to the invoice

187

To implement the same logic in GraphQL we must think in terms of mutations. A mutation has the following traits:

- It's not a query

- It takes arguments

We already saw how a GraphQL query with arguments looks. A mutation is not so different. With the requirements for creating a new invoice in mind, we want to be able to craft the mutation shown in Listing 11-15.

Listing 11-15. The Mutation Request for Creating a New Invoice

```
mutation {
 invoiceCreate(invoice: {
   user: 1
   date: "2021-02-15"
   dueDate: "2021-02-15"
   state: PAID
   items: [{
     quantity: 1
     description: "Django backend"
     price: 6000.00
     taxed: false
   },
   {
     quantity: 1
     description: "React frontend"
     price: 8000.00
     taxed: false
   }]
 }) {
   user { id }
   date
   state
 }
}
```

We can see from the invoice argument that the payload is not a simple scalar anymore, but a complex object. Such an input object is known as *input type*, that is, a strongly typed argument. We could pass these arguments separately in the signature of the mutation, but better, we can leverage GraphQL type system to define the shape of a single object as an argument. As a return value from this query, we ask the server to respond with the following data:

- The user ID connected to the new invoice

- The date and the state of the invoice

The process of adding a mutation in GraphQL is not dissimilar from adding queries:

- First we define the mutation and its inputs in the schema

- Then we create a resolver to handle the side effect

In GraphQL, mutations are declared under the `Mutation` type. To create our first mutation, add the code in Listing 11-16 to `billing/schema.graphql`.

Listing 11-16. billing/schema.graphql - The Mutation for Creating a New Invoice

```
type Mutation {
    invoiceCreate(invoice: InvoiceInput!): Invoice!
}
```

The `invoiceCreate` mutation takes an argument named `invoice`, of type `InvoiceInput`, non-nullable. In exchange, it returns a non-nullable `Invoice`. We now need to define input types. What they should look like? First of all, they should contain all the required fields for creating an invoice. Let's also not forget that item lines are an array of items. In `billing/schema.graphql`, we create two input types, as in Listing 11-17.

Listing 11-17. billing/schema.graphql - Input Types for the Mutation

```
input ItemLineInput {
    quantity: Int!
    description: String!
    price: Float!
    taxed: Boolean!
}
```

```
input InvoiceInput {
    user: ID!
    date: String!
    dueDate: String!
    state: InvoiceState
    items: [ItemLineInput!]!
}

type Mutation {
    invoiceCreate(invoice: InvoiceInput!): Invoice!
}
```

We now have:

- InvoiceInput: The input type used as the argument type for the mutation. It has an items array of ItemLineInput.

- ItemLineInput: The input type that represents a single item, as an input type.

These input types will be reflected in the schema and in the documentation. With the schema in place, we can now wire up the corresponding resolver.

Note   After making changes to billing/schema.graphql, you should restart Django development server, otherwise the changes won't be picked up.

Adding a Resolver for the Mutation

With the definition of the mutation in place, we can now add the corresponding resolver.

This resolver will touch the database to save a new invoice. To make this work, we need to introduce a bit more code in our schema, specifically:

- MutationType: To create a Mutation root type

- Invoice and ItemLine: The Django models

Listing 11-18 shows the changes we need to make in billing/schema.py.

Listing 11-18. billing/schema.py - Adding a Resolver to Fulfill the Mutation

```
...
from ariadne import ObjectType, MutationType
...
from billing.models import Invoice, ItemLine
...
mutation = MutationType()

@mutation.field("invoiceCreate")
def resolve_invoice_create(obj, info, invoice):
    user_id = invoice.pop("user")
    items = invoice.pop("items")

    invoice = Invoice.objects.create(user_id=user_id, **invoice)
    for item in items:
        ItemLine.objects.create(invoice=invoice, **item)
    return invoice

schema = make_executable_schema(type_defs, query, mutation)
```

A lot is going on in this code. Let's break it down:

- We use MutationType() to create a new mutation root type in Ariadne

- We decorate the mutation resolver so that it maps to the field defined in the schema

- In the resolver, we create a new invoice with the ORM

- We bind the mutation to the schema

Django wants an instance of the user to create a new invoice, but all we have from the GraphQL request is the ID of the user. This is why we remove user from the payload to pass it as user_id to Invoice.objects.create(). As for the next steps, the logic resembles what we did in Chapter 5 in the serializer. With this additional code in place, we can now send the mutation shown in Listing 11-19 to GraphQL.

Listing 11-19. The Mutation Request for Creating a New Invoice

```
mutation {
 invoiceCreate(invoice: {
   user: 1
   date: "2021-02-15"
   dueDate: "2021-02-15"
   state: PAID
   items: [{
     quantity: 1
     description: "Django backend"
     price: 6000.00
     taxed: false
   },
   {
     quantity: 1
     description: "React frontend"
     price: 8000.00
     taxed: false
   }]
 }) {
   user { id }
   date
   state
 }
}
```

Send out the mutation in the GraphQL Playground and you should see the following error:

```
Invoice() got an unexpected keyword argument 'dueDate'
```

This comes from the ORM layer of Django. In our mutation, we are sending out a field named dueDate, which is by convention in the GraphQL/JS world in camel case. However, Django expects due_date, as it's defined in the model. To fix this mismatch we can use convert_kwargs_to_snake_case from Ariadne. Open billing/schema.py and apply the change shown in Listing 11-20.

Listing 11-20. billing/schema.py - Converting from Camel Case to Snake Case

```
...
from ariadne.utils import convert_kwargs_to_snake_case
...
...
@mutation.field("invoiceCreate")
@convert_kwargs_to_snake_case
def resolve_invoice_create(obj, info, invoice):
...
```

Here, we decorate our mutation resolver with the converter utility. If everything is in the right spot, the server should now return the following response:

```
{
  "data": {
    "invoiceCreate": {
      "user": {
        "id": "1",
        "email": "juliana@acme.io"
      },
      "date": "2021-02-15",
      "state": "PAID"
    }
  }
}
```

With the query and the mutation in place, we are now ready to connect a React frontend to our GraphQL backend. But first, a word about GraphQL clients.

Introduction to GraphQL Clients

We saw that as far the network layer is concerned, GraphQL does not seem to require arcane tooling.

The conversation between a GraphQL client and its server happens over HTTP, with POST requests. We could even call a GraphQL service with curl. This means, in the browser we can use fetch, axios, or even XMLHttpRequest to make requests against a GraphQL API. In reality, this could work well for tiny apps, but sooner or later, in the real-world we need more than `fetch`. Specifically, for almost every data-fetching layer, we need to take into account some kind of caching. Thanks to the way GraphQL works, we can request only a subset of the data, but this does not rule out the need for sparing round trips to the server. In the next sections we work with one of the most popular GraphQL clients for JavaScript: Apollo Client. This tool abstracts away all the mundane details of performance optimization for developers working with GraphQL in the frontend.

Building the React Frontend

In Chapter 6, we built a Vue.js app for creating invoices.

The app has a `<form>`, which in turn contains a `<select>` and a number of fields for inserting invoice details. For this React app, we build the same structure, this time splitting each sub-component in its own file. In this chapter, we work with the query part. In Chapter 12, we see how to work with mutations. To start off we initialize a React project. We move to the `billing` folder, and we launch `create-react-app`. To create the React project, run the following command:

```
npx create-react-app react_spa --template typescript
```

This will create the project in `billing/react_spa`. Once the project is in place, in a new terminal move into the folder:

```
cd react_spa
```

From this folder we will start the React application as soon as the GraphQL layer is in place.

Note   For the React part, we work in `decoupled_dj/billing/react_spa`. Each proposed file must be created or change in the appropriate subfolder, starting from this path.

Getting Started with Apollo Client

To start off, we need to install Apollo Client in our project.

To do so, run the following command:

```
npm i @apollo/client
```

Once the installation is done, open `src/App.tsx`, wipe out all the boilerplate, and populate the file with the code shown in Listing 11-21.

Listing 11-21. src/App.tsx - Initializing Apollo Client

```
import {
ApolloClient,
InMemoryCache,
gql,
} from "@apollo/client";
const client = new ApolloClient({
uri: "http://127.0.0.1:8000/billing/graphql/",
cache: new InMemoryCache(),
});
```

Here we initialize the client by providing the URL of our GraphQL service. The `ApolloClient` constructor takes at least these two options:

- `uri`: The GraphQL service address

- `cache`: The caching strategy for the client

Here we use `InMemoryCache`, which is the default caching package included in Apollo Client. Once we have a client instance, to send requests to the server, we can use:

- `client.query()` to send queries

- `client.mutate()` to send mutations

For the usage with React, Apollo offers also a set of convenient hooks. In the next sections we create three React components, and we see how to work with client methods, and later with hooks.

Creating a Select Component

The <select> is part of our form, and will receive props from the outside. It should render an <option> element for each user in the database. In src/Select.tsx, we create the component shown in Listing 11-22.

Listing 11-22. src/Select.tsx - Select Component with TypeScript Definitions

```
import React from "react";

type Props = {
 id: string;
 name: string;
 options: Array<{
   id: string;
   email: string;
 }>;
};

const Select = ({ id, name, options }: Props) => {
 return (
   <select id={id} name={name} required={true}>
     <option value="">---</option>
     {options.map((option) => {
       return (
         <option value={option.id}>{option.email}</option>
       );
     })}
   </select>
 );
};

export default Select;
```

This component accepts from the outside a list of options to render out to the user. Before adding GraphQL, in Vue.js we were fetching this data from the REST API. In this app instead, we let a root component handle the data fetching, this time from a GraphQL service, and pass the data to the <select>. Let's now build the form.

Creating a Form Component

The form component is rather simple, as it accepts a function for handling the submit event, alongside one or more children. In src/Form.tsx, we create the component shown in Listing 11-23.

Listing 11-23. src/Form.tsx - Form Component with TypeScript Definitions

```
import React from "react";

type Props = {
 children: React.ReactNode;
 handleSubmit(
    event: React.FormEvent<HTMLFormElement>
 ): void;
};

const Form = ({ children, handleSubmit }: Props) => {
 return <form onSubmit={handleSubmit}>{children}</form>;
};

export default Form;
```

With the <form> and the <select> in place, we can now wire up the root component that will contain both.

Creating the Root Component and Making Queries

Each React app must have a root component, which in charge of rendering the shell of the whole app. To keep things simple, we will create the root component in src/App.tsx. In our root component, we need to:

- Query the GraphQL service for a list of clients, with a query

- Handle the submit event, with a mutation

The idea here is that when the app mounts, we use `useEffect()` to query the GraphQL API with `client.query()`. In the GraphQL Playground, we used the following query to get a list of clients:

```
query {
 getClients {
   id
   email
 }
}
```

In our React component we will use the same query to fetch clients. This is also the source of data for our `<select>`. The only thing to keep in mind when assembling the query is that this is an anonymous query, while in our React component we need to use a slightly different form, as a named query. Let's create the component in `src/App.tsx`, as in Listing 11-24.

Listing 11-24. src/App.tsx - React Component for Fetching Data

```
import React, { useEffect, useState } from "react";
import {
 ApolloClient,
 InMemoryCache,
 gql,
} from "@apollo/client";
import Form from "./Form";
import Select from "./Select";

const client = new ApolloClient({
 uri: "http://127.0.0.1:8000/billing/graphql/",
 cache: new InMemoryCache(),
});

const App = () => {
 const [options, setOptions] = useState([
   { id: "", email: "" },
 ]);
```

```
const handleSubmit = (
  event: React.FormEvent<HTMLFormElement>
) => {
  event.preventDefault();
  // client.mutate()
};

const GET_CLIENTS = gql`
  query getClients {
    getClients {
      id
      email
    }
  }
`;

useEffect(() => {
  client
    .query({
      query: GET_CLIENTS,
    })
    .then((queryResult) => {
      setOptions(queryResult.data.getClients);
    })
    .catch((error) => {
      console.log(error);
    });
}, []);

return (
  <Form handleSubmit={handleSubmit}>
    <Select id="user" name="user" options={options} />
  </Form>
);
};

export default App;
```

Let's explain in detail what is inside this code:

- We keep the logic for Apollo Client

- We use useState() to initialize the state for the component

- The state contains a list of options for the <select>, passed as props

- We define a minimal method for handling the submit event

- We use useEffect() to fetch data from the GraphQL API

- We render Form and Select to the user

It's also worth going through the Apollo part. First, the query is shown in Listing 11-25.

Listing 11-25. Building the Query

```
...
const GET_CLIENTS = gql`
  query getClients {
    getClients {
      id
      email
    }
  }
`;
...
```

Here we use gql to wrap the query in a template literal tag. This will generate a GraphQL Abstract syntax tree, which is used by the actual GraphQL client. Next up, let's examine the logic for sending the query:

```
...
  client
    .query({,
      query: GET_CLIENTS,
    })
    .then((queryResult) => {
      setOptions(queryResult.data.getClients);
    })
```

```
      .catch((error) => {
        console.log(error);
      });
...
```

In this logic, we call `client.query()` by providing an object with a `query` property, which gets assigned the previous query. `client.query()` returns a promise. This means we can use `then()` to consume the result, and `catch()` to handle errors. Inside `then()` we access the query result, and we use `setOptions` from the component state to save the result. The query result is accessible on `data.getClients`, which happens to be the name of our query. This looks a bit verbose. In fact, Apollo offers a `useQuery()` hook to reduce the boilerplate, as we will see in a moment. With everything saved, to test things out we should run Django, as usual in a terminal from `decoupled-dj`:

`python manage.py runserver`

In the other terminal, from `/billing/react_spa` we can run the React app:

`npm start`

This will launch React at `http://localhost:3000/`. In the UI, we should be able to see a `select` element, where each option renders the ID and the email of each client, as in Figure 11-3.

Figure 11-3. *The select component receives data from the GraphQL API*

This might not look like a tremendous achievement, not so different from fetching data with axios or fetch. In the next section, we see how to clean up the logic with Apollo Hooks for React.

Using Apollo Hooks for React

Apollo Client does not discourage the use of client.query().

However, in React applications, developers might want to use Apollo Hooks to keep the codebase consistent, much like we are accustomed to reaching for useState() and useEffect() in our components. Apollo Client includes a set of hooks that make working with GraphQL a breeze in React. To make queries, we can use the useQuery() hook instead of client.query(). However, this needs a bit of rearrangement in our application. First off, we need to wrap the whole app with ApolloProvider. For those familiar with Redux or the React Context API, this is the same concept exposed by Redux Provider or by the React Context counterpart. In our app, we first need to move Apollo Client instantiation in src/index.tsx. In this same file, we also wrap the whole app with the provider. Listing 11-26 illustrates the changes we need to make.

Listing 11-26. src/index.tsx - The App Shell

```
import React from "react";
import ReactDOM from "react-dom";
import {
 ApolloClient,
 InMemoryCache,
 ApolloProvider,
} from "@apollo/client";
import App from "./App";

const client = new ApolloClient({
 uri: "http://127.0.0.1:8000/billing/graphql/",
 cache: new InMemoryCache(),
});

ReactDOM.render(
 <React.StrictMode>
   <ApolloProvider client={client}>
     <App />
   </ApolloProvider>
 </React.StrictMode>,
 document.getElementById("root")
);
```

Now, in src/App.tsx we import only gql and useQuery from Apollo Client, plus we arrange the query a bit by moving it outside the component. In the component body instead we use useQuery(), as in Listing 11-27.

Listing 11-27. src/App.tsx - GraphQL Query with Apollo Hook

```
import React from "react";
import { gql, useQuery } from "@apollo/client";
import Form from "./Form";
import Select from "./Select";

const GET_CLIENTS = gql`
 query getClients {
   getClients {
     id
     email
   }
 }
`;

const App = () => {
 const { loading, data } = useQuery(GET_CLIENTS);

 const handleSubmit = (
   event: React.FormEvent<HTMLFormElement>
 ) => {
   event.preventDefault();
   // client.mutate()
 };

 return loading ? (
   <p>Loading ...</p>
 ) : (
   <Form handleSubmit={handleSubmit}>
     <Select
       id="user"
       name="user"
       options={data.getClients}
     />
```

```
    </Form>
  );
};
```

```
export default App;
```

Both `Form` and `Select` can stay the same. We can also notice that `useQuery()` takes our query as an argument and gives back for free a `loading` Boolean, convenient for conditional rendering, and a `data` object which contains the query result. This is much cleaner than `client.query()`. If we run the project again, everything should still work as expected, with a `<select>` rendered in the UI. With this change we now take full advantage of the declarative style of hooks, paired with GraphQL.

Note It is a good moment to commit the changes you made so far and to push the work to your Git repo. You can find the source code for this chapter at `https://github.com/valentinogagliardi/decoupled-dj/tree/chapter_11_graphql_ariadne`.

Summary

This chapter augmented the billing app from Chapter 6 with a GraphQL API. You also saw how to connect React to a GraphQL backend. In the process you learned about:

- GraphQL building blocks

- Adding GraphQL to a Django project with Ariadne

- Connecting React to a GraphQL backend

In the next chapter, we continue our exploration of GraphQL in Django, with Strawberry, and we also add mutations to the mix.

Additional Resources

- Ariadne documentation

- GraphQL: Designing a Data Language

CHAPTER 12

GraphQL in Django with Strawberry

This chapter covers:

- Code-first GraphQL with Strawberry

- Asynchronous Django and GraphQL

- Mutations with Apollo Client

In the previous chapter, we introduced the concept of schema-first for GraphQL APIs with Ariadne.

We explored queries and Apollo Client. In this chapter, we switch to a code-first approach to build our GraphQL API with Strawberry. In the process, we add mutations in the frontend to the mix, and we learn how to work with asynchronous code in Django.

Note   The rest of this chapter assumes you are in the repo root `decoupled-dj`, with the Python virtual environment active and with `DJANGO_SETTINGS_MODULE` configured as `decoupled_dj.settings.development`.

Getting Started with Strawberry in Django

In the beginning, GraphQL was mainly targeted at JavaScript.

It's not a coincidence that most early implementations of GraphQL servers were written for Node.js. In time, most programming communities picked up interest in this new paradigm for data querying, and these days we have a GraphQL implementation in most languages. In the Python land, we explored Ariadne and we mentioned Graphene.

© Valentino Gagliardi 2021
V. Gagliardi, *Decoupled Django*, https://doi.org/10.1007/978-1-4842-7144-5_12

What makes Strawberry different from these libraries? First off, Strawberry uses Python dataclasses heavily. Dataclasses in Python are a simple way to declare concise classes with attributes and optional logic. The following example shows a Python dataclass:

```
class User:
    name: str
    email: str
```

In this example, we declared a Python class with no behavior, but with two attributes, name and email. These attributes are also strongly typed; that is, they are able to enforce the kind of type they can hold, which is strings in this case. Strawberry makes heavy use of Python type hints. Type hints are an optional Python feature that can improve the robustness of our code. Python, much like JavaScript, is a dynamic language that does not enforce static types. With type hints, we can add a type layer to our Python code, which can be checked with a tool named MyPy before releasing the code in production. This can catch nasty bugs that could make their way to the runtime environment. Additionally, static type checks improve the developer experience. In Strawberry, we will use dataclasses to define our GraphQL types and type hints all along the way. Time to practice!

Installing Strawberry

To start off, we install Strawberry in our Django project:

```
pip install strawberry-graphql
```

After the installation, we update requirements/base.txt to include the new dependency. Next up, we enable Strawberry in decoupled_dj/settings/base.py, as shown in Listing 12-1.

Listing 12-1. decoupled_dj/settings/base.py - Enabling Strawberry in INSTALLED_APPS

```
INSTALLED_APPS = [
    ...
    "strawberry.django",
]
```

With Strawberry enabled, we can move to refactoring the schema from schema-first to code-first.

Designing the GraphQL Schema in Strawberry

In the previous chapter, we created a GraphQL schema in a `.graphql` file.

Let's recap what we have so far. Listing 12-2 shows the GraphQL schema we assembled in Chapter 11.

Listing 12-2. billing/schema.graphql - The Original GraphQL Schema

```
enum InvoiceState {
    PAID
    UNPAID
    CANCELLED
}

type User {
    id: ID
    name: String
    email: String
}

type Invoice {
    user: User
    date: String
    dueDate: String
    state: InvoiceState
    items: [ItemLine]
}

type ItemLine {
    quantity: Int
    description: String
    price: Float
    taxed: Boolean
}

type Query {
    getClients: [User]
    getClient(id: ID!): User
}
```

```
input ItemLineInput {
    quantity: Int!
    description: String!
    price: Float!
    taxed: Boolean!
}

input InvoiceInput {
    user: ID!
    date: String!
    dueDate: String!
    state: InvoiceState
    items: [ItemLineInput!]!
}

type Mutation {
    invoiceCreate(invoice: InvoiceInput!): Invoice!
}
```

In this schema, we used most of the GraphQL scalar types the language has to offer, plus our custom types and input types definitions. We also created two queries and a mutation. To appreciate what Strawberry has to offer, let's port each element of our schema from a plain text schema to Python code.

Types and Enums in Strawberry

To start off we begin with the base types of our GraphQL schema.

We need to declare User, Invoice, and ItemLine. To create the schema, open billing/schema.py, wipe out all the code we created in Chapter 11, and import the modules shown in Listing 12-3.

Listing 12-3. billing/schema.py - Initial Imports

```
import strawberry
import datetime
import decimal

from typing import List
```

typing is the main Python module from which we can peruse the most common type declarations. Next is strawberry itself. We also need the decimal module and the quintessential datetime. Next up, we are ready to create our first types. Listing 12-4 shows three GraphQL types in Strawberry.

Listing 12-4. billing/schema.py - First Types in Strawberry

```python
import strawberry
import datetime
import decimal

from typing import List

@strawberry.type
class User:
    id: strawberry.ID
    name: str
    email: str

@strawberry.type
class Invoice:
    user: User
    date: datetime.date
    due_date: datetime.date
    state: InvoiceState
    items: List["ItemLine"]

@strawberry.type
class ItemLine:
    quantity: int
    description: str
    price: decimal.Decimal
    taxed: bool
```

For someone new to Python typings, there a lot of things here that need a bit of explanation. Thankfully, Python is expressive enough to not overcomplicate things. Let's start from the top.

To declare a new GraphQL type in Strawberry we use the @strawberry.type decorator, which goes on top of our dataclasses. Next, each type is declared as a dataclass, each containing a set of attributes. In Chapters 1 and 11, we saw GraphQL scalar types. In Strawberry there isn't anything special to describe these scalars, apart from strawberry.ID. As you can see in Listing 12-4, most scalar types are represented as Python primitives: str, int, and bool. The only exception to this are the types for date and due_date, which we declared as strings in the original GraphQL schema. Since types in Strawberry are dataclasses, and dataclasses are "just" Python code, instead of strings for our date, we can now use datetime.date objects. This was one of our unsolved problems in Chapter 11, and it's now fixed.

Note   You may wonder what's the deal with due_date here and dueDate from the previous chapter. In the original GraphQL schema, we used dueDate in camel case. Ariadne converts this syntax to snake case before it reaches the Django ORM. Now we use snake case again in the GraphQL schema. Why? Being Python code, the convention is to use snake case for longish variables and function names. But this time, the conversion happens the other way around: in the GraphQL documentation schema, Strawberry will display the field as camel case!

Moving forward, notice how the relations are described by associating the dataclass attribute with the corresponding entity, like the User dataclass assigned to user in Invoice. Also note that the List type from Python typings to associate ItemLine to items. Previously, we used the Float scalar from GraphQL for the price of each ItemLine. In Python, we can use a more appropriate decimal.Decimal. Even from a simple listing like this, we can deduce that the Strawberry approach to writing GraphQL schemas as Python code brings a lot of benefits, including type safety, flexibility, and better handling of scalar types.

In the original GraphQL schema, we had an enum type associated with Invoice, which specifies whether the invoice is paid, unpaid, or cancelled. In the new schema we already have Invoice, so it's a matter of adding the enum. In Strawberry, we can use plain Python enums to declare the corresponding GraphQL type. In the schema file, add the enumeration, as in Listing 12-5 (this should go before User).

CHAPTER 12   GRAPHQL IN DJANGO WITH STRAWBERRY

Listing 12-5. billing/schema.py - Enum Type in Strawberry

```
...
from enum import Enum

@strawberry.enum
class InvoiceState(Enum):
    PAID = "PAID"
    UNPAID = "UNPAID"
    CANCELLED = "CANCELLED"
...
```

This is quite similar to the choices for our Invoice model in Django. With a bit of creativity, one could reuse this Strawberry enum in the Django model (or the other way around). With the enum in place, we are almost ready to test things out. Let's add resolvers and queries in the next sections.

Working with Resolvers (Again)

We already learned that a GraphQL schema needs resolvers to return data.

Let's add two resolvers to our schema, copied almost straight from Chapter 11 (see Listing 12-6).

Listing 12-6. billing/schema.py - Adding Resolvers to the Schema

```
...
from users.models import User as UserModel
...

def resolve_clients():
    return UserModel.objects.all()

def resolve_client(id: strawberry.ID):
    return UserModel.objects.get(id=id)
```

To avoid clashing with the User GraphQL type here, we import our user model as UserModel. Next up, we declare resolvers to fulfill the original GraphQL queries, namely getClient and getClients. Notice how we pass an id as the argument to the

213

second resolver to fetch a single user by ID as we did in the previous chapter. With these resolvers in place we can add a Query type and finally wire up the GraphQL endpoint in the next section.

Queries in Strawberry and Wiring Up the GraphQL Endpoint

With the fundamental types and the resolvers in place, we can create a code-first Query type for our API.

Add the code shown in Listing 12-7 to the schema file.

Listing 12-7. billing/schema.py - Adding a Root Query Type

```
@strawberry.type
class Query:
    get_clients: List[User] = strawberry.field(resolver=resolve_clients)
    get_client: User = strawberry.field(resolver=resolve_client)
schema = strawberry.Schema(query=Query)
```

Here we are telling Strawberry that there's a Query type for GraphQL with two fields. Let's look at these fields in detail:

- get_clients returns a list of Users and is connected to the resolver named resolve_clients

- get_client returns a single User and is connected to the resolver named resolve_client

Both resolvers are wrapped with strawberry.field(). Notice that both queries will be converted to camel case in the GraphQL documentation, even though they are declared as snake case in our code. In the last line we load our schema into Strawberry, so it is picked up and served to the user. It is important to note that resolvers in Strawberry don't have to be disconnected from the Query dataclass itself. In fact, we could have declared them as methods in the Query. We leave these two resolvers outside of the dataclass, but we will see mutations as methods of the Mutation dataclass in a moment.

With this logic in place, we can connect the GraphQL layer to the Django URL system in `billing/urls.py`. Remove the GraphQL view from Ariadne. This time, instead of a regular view, we use the asynchronous GraphQL view from Strawberry, as shown in Listing 12-8.

Listing 12-8. billing/urls.py - Wiring Up the GraphQL Endpoint

```
...
from strawberry.django.views import AsyncGraphQLView
...

app_name = "billing"

urlpatterns = [
    ...
    path("graphql/",
        AsyncGraphQLView.as_view(schema=schema),
        name="graphql"
        ),
]
```

By running the GraphQL API asynchronously, we have a world of new possibilities, but a lot of new things to think about as well, as we will see in a moment. We explore an example in the next sections. Remember that to run Django asynchronously, we need an ASG-capable server like Uvicorn. We installed this package in Chapter 5, but to recap, you can install Uvicorn with the following command:

```
pip install uvicorn
```

Next, export the `DJANGO_SETTINGS_MODULE` environment variable if you haven't already:

```
export DJANGO_SETTINGS_MODULE=decoupled_dj.settings.development
```

Finally, run the server with the following command:

```
uvicorn decoupled_dj.asgi:application --reload
```

The `--reload` flag ensures that Uvicorn reloads on file changes. If everything goes well, you should see the following output:

```
INFO: Uvicorn running on http://127.0.0.1:8000 (Press CTRL+C to quit)
```

Throughout the next sections, we will run Django under Uvicorn. Now we can head over to `http://127.0.0.1:8000/billing/graphql/`. This should open GraphiQL, a playground for exploring the GraphQL API. In the playground, we can send out queries and mutations and explore the schema and the integrated documentation, just as we did with Ariadne. Now that you have the big picture, you can complete the schema with input types and mutations.

Input Types and Mutations in Strawberry

We saw that input types in GraphQL are basically arguments for a mutation.

To define an input type in Strawberry, we still create a dataclass, but this time we use the `@strawberry.input` decorator on top of it. Let's create two input types for `ItemLineInput` and `InvoiceInput` (this code can go after the `Query` type); see Listing 12-9.

Listing 12-9. billing/schema.py - Adding Input Types to the Schema

```
...
@strawberry.input
class ItemLineInput:
    quantity: int
    description: str
    price: decimal.Decimal
    taxed: bool

@strawberry.input
class InvoiceInput:
    user: strawberry.ID
    date: datetime.date
    due_date: datetime.date
    state: InvoiceState
    items: List[ItemLineInput]
```

Here we have dataclasses with the appropriate attribute for the input type. As the icing, ... oops, strawberry, on the cake, let's add a mutation as well (see Listing 12-10).

Listing 12-10. billing/schema.py - Adding a Mutation to the Schema

```
...
import dataclasses
...
from billing.models import Invoice as InvoiceModel
from billing.models import ItemLine as ItemLineModel
...
@strawberry.type
class Mutation:
    @strawberry.mutation
    def create_invoice(self, invoice: InvoiceInput) -> Invoice:
        _invoice = dataclasses.asdict(invoice)
        user_id = _invoice.pop("user")
        items = _invoice.pop("items")
        state = _invoice.pop("state")

        new_invoice = InvoiceModel.objects.create(
            user_id=user_id, state=state.value, **_invoice
        )
        for item in items:
            ItemLineModel.objects.create(invoice=_invoice, **item)
        return new_invoice

schema = strawberry.Schema(query=Query, mutation=Mutation)
```

This code bears a bit of explanation. First off, we import our Django models again, this time by aliasing them to avoid clashes with the dataclasses. Next up, we define a Mutation and a method inside it. The method, named create_invoice(), takes InvoiceInput input type as a parameter and is decorated with @strawberry.mutation. Inside the method we convert the dataclass input type to a dictionary. This is important because the mutation parameter is a dataclass, not a dictionary. This way, we can pop out the keys we need, as we did with Ariadne. In the mutation, we also pop out state, which is later passed as state.value to InvoiceModel.objects.create(). At the time of this writing, Strawberry doesn't convert automatically enums keys to strings, so we need to do a bit of data drilling. Finally, notice the type annotation for the return value of this mutation, Invoice. At the very end of the file we also load the mutation dataclass into the schema.

Mutation and input types complete our GraphQL schema for now. At this stage we could use the GraphiQL Playground to send an `invoiceCreate` mutation, but instead of trying things manually, we will implement the mutation in our React frontend. But first, let's look at the implications of running Strawberry asynchronously with Django.

Working Asynchronously with the Django ORM

After setting everything up, you might have noticed that by sending even a simple query in GraphiQL, everything blows up.

Even by sending out a simple query, Django will respond with the following error:

```
You cannot call this from an async context - use a thread or sync_to_async.
```

The error is a bit cryptic, but this comes from the ORM layer. At the time of writing, Django's ORM isn't async-ready yet. This means we can't simply launch ORM queries while running Django asynchronously. To work around the issue we need to wrap ORM interactions with an asynchronous adapter called `sync_to_async` from ASGI. To keep things digestible, we first move the actual ORM queries into separate functions. Then, we wrap these functions with `sync_to_async`. Listing 12-11 shows the required changes.

Listing 12-11. billing/schema.py - Converting ORM Queries to Work Asynchronously

```
...
from asgiref.sync import sync_to_async
...

def _get_all_clients():
    return list(UserModel.objects.all())

async def resolve_clients():
    return await sync_to_async(_get_all_clients)()

def _get_client(id):
    return UserModel.objects.get(id=id)

async def resolve_client(id: strawberry.ID):
    return await sync_to_async(_get_client)(id)
```

Let's look at what is going on here. First off, we move the ORM logic to two regular functions. In the first function, `_get_all_clients()`, we fetch all the clients from the database with `.all()`. We also force Django to evaluate the queryset by converting it to a list with `list()`. It's necessary to evaluate the query in the asynchronous context, because Django querysets are lazy by default. In the second function, `_get_client()`, we simply get a single user from the database. Both functions are then called in two asynchronous functions, wrapped in `sync_to_async()`. This machinery will make ORM code work under ASGI.

Resolvers are not the only piece that needs the async wrapper. While at this stage, we don't expect anybody to hit our GraphQL mutation furiously, the ORM code for saving new invoices needs to be wrapped too. Again, we can pull out the ORM-related code to separate functions and then wrap these with `sync_to_async`, as shown in Listing 12-12.

Listing 12-12. billing/schema.py - Converting ORM Queries to Work Asynchronously

```
...
from asgiref.sync import sync_to_async
...
def _create_invoice(user_id, state, invoice):
    return InvoiceModel.objects.create(user_id=user_id, state=state.value,
    **invoice)

def _create_itemlines(invoice, item):
    ItemLineModel.objects.create(invoice=invoice, **item)

@strawberry.type
class Mutation:
    @strawberry.mutation
    async def create_invoice(self, invoice: InvoiceInput) -> Invoice:
        _invoice = dataclasses.asdict(invoice)
        user_id = _invoice.pop("user")
        items = _invoice.pop("items")
        state = _invoice.pop("state")

        new_invoice = await sync_to_async(_create_invoice)(user_id, state,
        _invoice)
```

```
    for item in items:
        await sync_to_async(_create_itemlines)(new_invoice, item)
    return new_invoice
```

This might seem like a lot of code to do something that Django provides out-of-the-box, namely SQL queries, but this is the price to pay at this moment in order to run Django asynchronously. In the future, we hope to have better async support for the ORM layer. For now, with these changes, we are ready to run Strawberry and Django side by side asynchronously. We can now move to the frontend to implement mutations with Apollo Client.

Working Again on the Frontend

In Chapter 11, we began to work on a React/TypeScript frontend, which acted as a client for our GraphQL API.

So far, we implemented a simple query in the frontend for a `<select>` component. First, we worked with Apollo `client.query()`, which is a lowish-level method for making queries. Then, we refactored to use the `useQuery()` hook. In the following sections, we tackle mutations in the frontend with Apollo Client and `useMutation()`.

Note   For the React part, we work in `decoupled_dj/billing/react_spa`. Each proposed file must be created or changed in the appropriate subfolder, starting from this path.

Creating Invoices with a Mutation

We left the previous chapter with the App component shown in Listing 12-13.

Listing 12-13. src/App.tsx - GraphQL Query with Apollo

```
import React from "react";
import { gql, useQuery } from "@apollo/client";
import Form from "./Form";
import Select from "./Select";
```

```
const GET_CLIENTS = gql`
 query getClients {
   getClients {
     id
     email
   }
 }
`;

const App = () => {
 const { loading, data } = useQuery(GET_CLIENTS);

 const handleSubmit = (
   event: React.FormEvent<HTMLFormElement>
 ) => {
   event.preventDefault();
   // client.mutate()
 };

 return loading ? (
   <p>Loading ...</p>
 ) : (
   <Form handleSubmit={handleSubmit}>
     <Select
       id="user"
       name="user"
       options={data.getClients}
     />
   </Form>
 );
};

export default App;
```

This component uses a query to populate the <select> as soon as it is mounted
in the DOM. It's now time to implement a mutation. So far in Ariadne, we sent out
mutations by providing the mutation payload in the GraphQL Playground. This time,
things change a bit in the frontend: we need to use useMutation() from Apollo Client.
First, we import the new hook, as shown in Listing 12-14.

Listing 12-14. src/App.tsx - Importing useMutation

```
...
import { gql, useQuery, useMutation } from "@apollo/client";
...
```

Next, right after the GET_CLIENTS query, we declare a mutation named CREATE_
INVOICE, as shown in Listing 12-15.

Listing 12-15. src/App.tsx - Declaring a Mutation

```
...
const CREATE_INVOICE = gql`
 mutation createInvoice($invoice: InvoiceInput!) {
   createInvoice(invoice: $invoice) {
     date
     state
   }
 }
`;
...
```

This mutation looks a bit like a function, as it takes a parameter and returns some data to the caller. But the parameter in this case is an input type. Now, in App we use the new hook. The usage of useMutation() recalls useState() from React: we can array-destructure a function from the hook. Listing 12-16 shows the mutation hook in our component.

Listing 12-16. src/App.tsx - Using the useMutation Hook

```
...
const App = () => {
 const { loading, data } = useQuery(GET_CLIENTS);
 const [createInvoice] = useMutation(CREATE_INVOICE);
...
```

In addition, we can also destructure an object with two properties: error and loading. As with the query, these will provide info in case of errors, and a loading state to conditionally render the UI during the mutation. To avoid clashing with loading from the query, we assign a new name to the mutation loader. Listing 12-17 shows the changes.

Listing 12-17. src/App.tsx - Using the useMutation Hook with Loading and Error

```
...
const App = () => {
  const { loading, data } = useQuery(GET_CLIENTS);
  const [
      createInvoice,
      { error, loading: mutationLoading },
  ] = useMutation(CREATE_INVOICE);
...
```

Now that we've met mutations, let's see how to use them in the frontend. From the useMutation() hook, we destructured createInvoice(), a function that we can now call in response to some user interaction. In this case we already have an handleSubmit() in our component, and that is a good place to send out a mutation to create new data into the database. It is important to note that the mutation will return a promise. This means we can use then()/catch()/finally() or try/catch/finally with async/await. What can we send in the mutation? More important, how can we use it? Once we get the mutator function from the hook, we can call it by providing an option object, which should contain at least the mutation variables. The following example illustrates how we can use this mutation:

```
...
  await createInvoice({
    variables: {
      invoice: {
        user: 1,
        date: "2021-05-01",
        dueDate: "2021-05-31",
        state: "UNPAID",
        items: [
          {
            description: "Django consulting",
            price: 7000,
```

```
            taxed: true,
            quantity: 1,
          },
        ],
      },
    },
  });
...
```

In this mutation, we send the entire input type for the mutation, as declared in our schema. In this example, we hardcode some data, but in the real world we might want to get mutation variables dynamically with JavaScript. This is exactly what we did in Chapter 6, when we built a POST payload from a form with FormData. Let's complete our form by adding the appropriate inputs and a Submit button. To start, Listing 12-18 shows the complete React form (for brevity, we skip any CSS and stylistic concerns here).

Listing 12-18. src/App.tsx - The Complete Form

```
<Form handleSubmit={handleSubmit}>
  <Select
    id="user"
    name="user"
    options={data.getClients}
  />
  <div>
    <label htmlFor="date">Date</label>
    <input id="date" name="date" type="date" required />
  </div>
  <div>
    <label htmlFor="dueDate">Due date</label>
    <input
      id="dueDate"
      name="dueDate"
      type="date"
      required
    />
  </div>
```

```
<div>
  <label htmlFor="quantity">Qty</label>
  <input
    id="quantity"
    name="quantity"
    type="number"
    min="0"
    max="10"
    required
  />
</div>
<div>
  <label htmlFor="description">Description</label>
  <input
    id="description"
    name="description"
    type="text"
    required
  />
</div>
<div>
  <label htmlFor="price">Price</label>
  <input
    id="price"
    name="price"
    type="number"
    min="0"
    step="0.01"
    required
  />
</div>
<div>
  <label htmlFor="taxed">Taxed</label>
  <input id="taxed" name="taxed" type="checkbox" />
</div>
```

```
{mutationLoading ? (
  <p>Creating the invoice ...</p>
) : (
  <button type="submit">CREATE INVOICE</button>
)}
</Form>
```

This form contains all the inputs for creating a new invoice. At the bottom, note the conditional rendering based on the state of `mutationLoading`.

This is a nice thing to have in order to inform the user about the state of request. With the form in place, we can assemble the logic for sending out the mutation from `handleSubmit()`. For convenience, we can use `async/await` with `try/catch`. Some words before looking at the code:

- We build the mutation payload starting from a `FormData`

- In the building logic, we convert `quantity` to an integer and `taxed` to a Boolean

These last steps are necessary because our GraphQL schema expects quantity to be an integer, while in the form it is simply a string. Listing 12-19 shows the complete code.

Listing 12-19. src/App.tsx - Logic for Sending the Mutation

```
const handleSubmit = async (
 event: React.FormEvent<HTMLFormElement>
) => {
 event.preventDefault();
 if (event.target instanceof HTMLFormElement) {
   const formData = new FormData(event.target);

   const invoice = {
     user: formData.get("user"),
     date: formData.get("date"),
     dueDate: formData.get("dueDate"),
     state: "UNPAID",
     items: [
       {
         quantity: parseInt(
```

```
        formData.get("quantity") as string
      ),
      description: formData.get("description"),
      price: formData.get("price"),
      taxed: Boolean(formData.get("taxed")),
    },
  ],
};

try {
  const { data } = await createInvoice({
    variables: { invoice },
  });
  event.target.reset();
} catch (error) {
  console.error(error);
}
}
};
```

Apart from the FormData logic, the rest is pretty straightforward:

- We send out the mutation with createInvoice() by providing an invoice payload

- If everything goes well, we reset the form with event.target. reset()

If we test things in the browser, we should be able to send out the mutation and get a response from the server. This process can be seen in the browser's console, as shown in Figure 12-1, where the Response tab is highlighted.

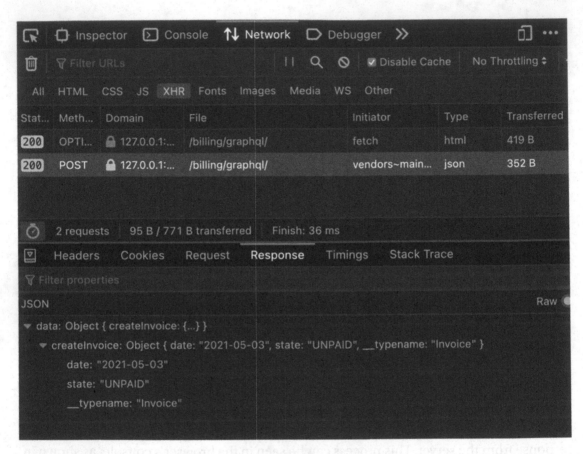

Figure 12-1. *The mutation response from the GraphQL server*

In REST, when we create or modify a resource with a POST or PATCH request, the API responds with a payload. GraphQL makes no exceptions. In fact, we can access the response data on the mutation, as shown in the following snippet:

```
const { data } = await createInvoice({
 variables: { invoice },
});
// do something with the data
```

In Figure 12-1, we can see the `data` object containing a property named `createInvoice`, which holds the fields we requested from the mutation. We can also see `__typename`. This is part of GraphQL's introspection capabilities, which make it possible to ask GraphQL "what type is this object"? An explanation of GraphQL introspection is out of the scope of this book, but the official documentation is a good starting point for learning more.

Note   It is a good moment to commit the changes you made so far and to push the work to your Git repo. You can find the source code for this chapter at `https://github.com/valentinogagliardi/decoupled-dj/tree/chapter_12_graphql_strawberry`.

What's Next?

We've barely scratched the surface of GraphQL in these last pages. The subject is bigger than two chapters. The following is a list of topics that you can explore on your own after finishing this book:

- *Authentication and deployment*: In fully decoupled setups, GraphQL works well with JWT tokens for authentication. However, the specification does not enforce any particular type of authentication method. This means it is possible to use session-based authentication for GraphQL API, as we saw in Chapter 10 for REST.

- *Subscriptions*: GraphQL Python libraries for Django can integrate with Django Channels to provide subscriptions over WebSocket.

- *Testing*: Testing GraphQL API does not involve any magic. Since they accept and return JSON, any testing HTTP client for Python or Django can be used to test a GraphQL endpoint.

- *Sorting, filtering, and pagination*: It's easy to sort, filter, and paginate responses with Django and the Django REST Framework tools. However, to implement the same things in GraphQL, we need to write a bit of code by hand. But since GraphQL queries accept arguments, it's not so hard to build custom filtering capabilities in a GraphQL API.

- *Performances:* Since queries in GraphQL can be nested, great care must be taken to avoid crashing our database with N+1 queries. Most GraphQL libraries include a so-called *dataloader*, which takes care of caching database queries.

EXERCISE 12-1: ADDING MORE ASYNCHRONOUS MUTATIONS

The wireframe in Chapter 6 has a Send Email button. Try to implement this logic in the React frontend, with a mutation. On the backend, you will also need a new asynchronous mutation to send the email.

EXERCISE 12-2: TESTING GRAPHQL

Add tests to this simple application: you can test the GraphQL endpoint with Django testing tools and test the interface with Cypress.

Summary

In this chapter, we closed the circle with the basics of GraphQL and asynchronous Django. You learned how to:

- Use GraphQL mutations in the backend and in the frontend

- Work with asynchronous Django

Now it's your turn! Go build your next Django project!

Additional Resources

- GraphQL-first Django

- GraphQL.org

Index

A

Ancillary JavaScript tools, 28
Ariadne
    installation, 174
    loading schema, 177–178
    template configuration, 174
Asynchronous code
    context manager, 39
    framework, 39
    httpx client, 38
    list_links(), 39
    synchronous view, 37
    task queue, 37

B

Billing app
    configuration, 63
    enable option, 66
    ER diagram, 65
    GraphQL schema, 175–176
    models, 64–66
    pseudo-decoupled
        approach, 68–80
    startapp command, 63
    wireframe, 66–68
Blog application
    enable process, 115–116
    fantastic framework, 113
    model building, 114–115

react (*see* React ecosystem)
serializers/views, 116–120

C

Class-based views (viewsets), 33–34
Code splitting, 20
Cross-Origin Resource Sharing (CORS),
    99–101
CRUD viewsets (DRF), 33–34
Cypress, 134

D, E

Decoupled application
    advantages, 4
    content repositories, 4
    hypermedia (*see* Hypermedia)
    JavaScript/HTML frontend, 3
    single-page applications, 4
    software engineering, 2
Deployment theory
    deployment, 108–111
    Gunicorn production
        requirements, 106
    NGINX configuration, 105–106
    production dependencies, 109
    server configuration, 105
    subdomain configuration, 107
    target machine, 104
    Vue.js production, 107–108

W, X, Y, Z

Printed in the United States
by Baker & Taylor Publisher Services